BLUE-COLLAR KAIZEN

Mack Story

ISBN-10: 154663908X
ISBN-13: 978-1546639084

DEDICATION

To those who truly have *respect for the people*.

CONTENTS

ACKNOWLEDGMENTS

I would like to thank Jim Noreault for believing in me and allowing me to accelerate my Lean journey in his plant.

Jim revealed to me that high impact leadership is more caught than taught.

1

CREATING A KAIZEN CULTURE

DEVELOP THE FRONT LINE
TO IMPROVE THE BOTTOM LINE

*"A truly Lean company develops all the people because
they are people with potential, not because they
are people with positions." ~ Mack Story*

When you are leading Lean, you are responsible for
creating the kaizen culture in your organization, regardless
of your position.

Anyone with a desire and a passion for Lean can lead
Lean. Whether it's the CEO or the front line supervisor,
someone must lead the way. Why shouldn't it be you?
You're investing time in developing yourself because you
want to be successful as a Lean leader and make a high
impact. I want to help you.

I'm going to help you increase your influence
throughout the organization starting with those on the
kaizen teams you lead. Leading kaizen teams effectively is
the perfect way to position yourself as the leader of the
people. When you invest in and develop the people, your
influence will spread far and wide among those people.

You don't have to be their boss to lead them. They
simply must choose to follow you. I've led thousands of
people who never reported to me, but they chose to
follow me. When people choose to follow you because of
who you are and what you represent, you are creating the
kaizen culture. You will develop tremendous influence.

Those who brought me into their organizations always hired a consultant to lead a team, but they always got a high impact Lean leader who transformed the culture. I didn't need a positon of authority to make things happen. I only needed a team.

In a kaizen culture, the people are engaged. They identify problems. They offer solutions. They take action. They respect their leaders and are respected by their leaders. They don't blame. They don't point fingers. They don't whine. They shine.

In a kaizen culture, people are growing because they want to. They are improving processes because they want to. They are participating on kaizen teams because they want to. They are making small changes because they want to. They are following the leader because they want to.

Accept responsibility for creating a kaizen culture and you will attract followers one kaizen team at a time. It is possible. I did it many times in many places always with great success.

Are you up for the challenge? It will be hard. You won't be successful without engaging, empowering, and encouraging the people.

I've heard numerous leaders in "Lean" organizations say, *"Lean is all about people."* They read it or heard it somewhere and thought it sounded good. So, they repeat it every chance they get, especially to customers. I think they believe saying it will make it so. For most of the leaders I've met, if they were being completely truthful, they would say, *"Lean is all about the people improving the processes, reducing the costs, and increasing the profits."*

What they don't realize is Lean is about leadership of the people. Leadership is the key to creating a true kaizen culture.

I know very few Lean leaders who study leadership. A few do, but most do not. If they read anything at all, it's usually books about the Lean tools. I focused on reading books about Lean tools too, until I realized respect for the people meant developing the people. To develop the people, you must be influencing and leading them. So, I put down the books about the Lean tools and picked up the books about leadership and influence.

I haven't looked back.

To create a kaizen culture, you must move beyond the tools and begin to focus intentionally on the people. Unfortunately, most organizations focus only on the tools and include the people because they need them to execute the Lean mission. It's not really about the people.

You are about to learn how to create a kaizen culture by making your kaizen events about the people. It will not only be fun, it will be rewarding. But, it won't be easy. Everything throughout this book will help you become the type of Lean leader who will naturally help create a kaizen culture.

I want to encourage you to begin to see each kaizen event as mini-culture within a culture. A kaizen culture is not only good for the people, but it is also created by the people.

"Leaders who don't appreciate Lean make the error of casting great visions and getting people excited but then falling back into command-and-control management. Lean traditionalists make the error of implementing Lean without a compelling vision, so that improvements are made but ultimately undermine the culture rather than galvanizing it."
~ Bob Chapman

2

LIVING KAIZEN

LIVE IT TO LEAD IT

"The one thing that separates high impact leaders from low impact leaders is CHARACTER. That one thing is made up of many things." ~ Mack Story

You will not learn about Lean tools in this book. You will learn about leading teams in a Lean environment while using values and principles to achieve amazing results.

Each chapter is about high impact Lean leadership. You *must* manage things and processes because they don't think or feel. But, you *should* lead people because they do.

Lean tools are related to improving the processes. High impact Lean leadership is related to respecting the people. The most important person you will ever lead is yourself. The degree to which you develop yourself determines the degree to which you will influence others.

You can't give what you don't have. You can't teach what you don't know. You can't model what you don't live. You won't have high impact influence without high impact character.

Everything I'm about to share with you will help you increase your influence with all people in all situations. High impact Lean leaders have a lot of influence. Low impact Lean leaders have very little influence.

Lean leadership is not about your title, your position, or your authority. Actually, those who struggle to lead

Lean the most are those who attempt to leverage their authority to get results. They are doomed from the start. Napoleon Hill said, *"One of the greatest leaders who ever lived stated the secret of his leadership in six words, as follows: 'Kindness is more powerful than compulsion.'"*

High impact Lean leadership is based on moral authority, not formal authority. It's about who you are: your character. It's not about what you are: your position or title.

Regardless of your position or title, to be a high impact Lean leader, you truly must have *respect for the people*. All of the people, at all times, at all levels, and in all departments.

Low impact Lean leaders *facilitate* kaizen events and *blame others* for their lack of results. High impact Lean leaders *lead* kaizen events and *accept responsibility* for achieving results.

After more than 11,000 hours of leading leaders and their cross-functional teams through all types of kaizen events and training many others to do so between 2005-2012, I know one thing for certain. To effectively lead Lean teams through change, you must authentically value people and have a hunger for initiating change for the better, not only in their lives at work and at home, but also in your own life.

I call this *living kaizen*: the endless, continuous pursuit of personal improvement. If we teach it, we should live it.

I began my manufacturing career in 1988 on the front lines of a manufacturing plant as an entry-level machine operator. In 1995, I started to climb my way up from the bottom. I grew through many positions including Process Engineer, Lean Manager, Lean Consultant, and now, author and motivational leadership speaker. More on my journey can be found in my first book, *Defining Influence:*

Increasing Your Influence Increases Your Options.

In 2005, I was working as a Process Engineer when the plant manager stopped by and asked me if I would be willing to accept responsibility for leading a plant wide 5S initiative as we started our Lean journey. I agreed without truly knowing what I was agreeing to.

He gave me 12 weeks. I started by creating eight teams that met several hours every week. During that 12 week period, I led 96 5S kaizen events. That's how my Lean journey began.

I define kaizen simply as continuous improvement or making many small changes for the better. There seem to be many varying definitions that basically mean the same thing: constantly strive to be better tomorrow than you are today. In two simple words, kaizen means *get better.*

You can get better personally and professionally. You can get better at home and at work. You can get better in the area of character: who you are. You can get better in the area of competence: what you know.

Mark Graban said, *"Training people and making lists of waste might create awareness, but we need the courage to take action and lead efforts to improve the system."* It starts with you. Do you have the courage to lead yourself better? Do you have the courage to lead others better?

When it comes to leading yourself and others, your character will launch you or limit you. Your character will determine if you're a low impact leader struggling to create positive change or if you're a high impact leader influencing many to embrace, support, leverage, and lead change throughout the organization.

Will you live kaizen? Will you achieve greater success?

"Your best chance for success is reading.
Learn to earn. Read to succeed." ~ Jeffrey Gitomer

3

OVERCOMING THE RESISTANCE

THE CHALLENGE OF CHANGE

"Managers, especially senior managers, overestimate their effectiveness, particularly as they seek to improve their organizations through formal initiatives. And, they underestimate the impact, often negative, of their daily personal actions on employees." ~ Jim Womack

For me, living kaizen took on a new meaning when I accepted responsibility for leading the 5S initiative in my plant in 2005. Nobody reported to me. Yet, I was responsible for leading (influencing) everybody down the Lean 5S path, including all of those with a formal position of authority. Lean leadership is about influence.

Soon after the plant manager asked me to lead the 5S initiative and to begin reporting directly to him, he resigned. We continued the 5S mission successfully without him. A few months later, we had a new plant manager, Jim Noreault. I soon found out that he was not only a plant manager. Jim was also a high impact Lean leader. He knew how to unleash our Lean potential.

When I volunteered to lead the 5S initiative, I didn't realize I would also be leading our complete Lean transformation. We all thought 5S was all we were going to do. We were a typical traditional batch & queue operation. Three short years into our Lean transformation, we had converted the entire plant into a cellular, single piece flow operation. We went from -3% gross profit margin to +35%. We achieved success!

That was impressive when you consider I had never led Lean, and there was always a lot of resistance at all levels. Very few of our 200 associates had ever heard of Lean. Very few of our formal authority leaders at any level knew much about Lean or wanted to learn about it.

I had never read a leadership book. Like most blue-collar organizations, we didn't conduct leadership development at any level within the plant. But, we did have a high impact leader in Jim Noreault.

Jim was a leader of leaders. He was the type of plant manager every Lean leader wants to report to. He was the type of top leader the Lean books say you must have in order to be successful, but the kind you seldom encounter in the real world.

Jim knew Lean started with him, but he also knew it wasn't about him. He let me find my way and own our Lean journey. He let me self-educate on the job as I read Lean books and experimented endlessly with our team.

I also read endlessly at home. Lean wasn't a job for me. It was my passion. I was leading and living kaizen.

Jim was always available to any of us. He was our biggest cheerleader. He gave me and everyone in the plant credit for all of our successes and for making it all happen. He mentored, coached, removed roadblocks, got involved, got dirty, laughed with us, and helped us battle the never-ending resistance to change. Jim cared.

There was A LOT of resistance as there usually is. With Jim's support, those of us who were bought-in to him and his vision went over it, around it, underneath it, through it, and sometimes, Jim removed it. We first tried to change the people (get them onboard). But, eventually if that didn't work, Jim changed the people (removed them and brought in someone who was a better fit).

Without Jim's leadership, our Lean transformation would have failed, as it always does without a high impact leader at the top.

In 2008, I resigned from my position and launched a process improvement consulting company. I also started studying leadership. From then on, I incorporated leadership development into all of the kaizen events I led.

I often told my teams, *"There's two ways to lead a Lean transformation: from the top down or the bottom up. Since I'm not the CEO, when we're on a team together, we're leading Lean with the people from the bottom up. Our mission is to get results and increase our influence."* As far as I was concerned, I was always leading Lean from the bottom up.

As a consultant, top leaders often brought me in to improve the process and increase the profits, not to grow and develop the people. I knew there would be resistance to change. Why? Because change is hard when you aren't growing and developing the people in an effort to prepare and engage the people.

You can overcome this resistance by increasing your influence with as many people in as many directions as you can from right where you are. You start by leading each team effectively and respecting the people. Lean leadership rises and falls on influence.

If there are challenges you can't overcome, the root cause is inside you, not outside you.

"Leadership is complicated. It has many facets: respect, experience, emotional strength, people skills, discipline, vision, momentum, timing- the list goes on. As you can see, many factors that come into play in leadership are intangible. That's why leaders require so much seasoning to be effective." ~ John C. Maxwell

4

DEFINING INFLUENCE

INFLUENCE TRUMPS AUTHORITY

"Lean managers seek responsibility to address important issues by leading as if they have no authority. Leading without the benefit of authority is actually critical in any organization because even in authority-based organizations managers rarely have control over everything touching a process."
~ Jim Womack

Womack was stating what I'll be teaching you throughout this book, *"You don't need authority to lead Lean. Influence will always trump authority."* High impact Lean leadership requires influence, but it doesn't require authority.

Phrases like, *"My hands are tied,"* or *"They don't report to me,"* or *"Those people won't do what I tell them,"* really mean, *"I don't have any influence, and I can't accomplish anything without it."*

You're holding in your hands a resource filled with tips and principles that will help you increase your influence (leadership) far beyond the influence that comes with a title or position.

Most often, I had more authentic influence in the plants I was supporting than most of the leaders with formal positions of authority. Because I invested in developing the people while leading kaizen teams, I built meaningful relationships throughout the entire facility.

I could make things happen when the leaders wouldn't even attempt to make them happen. I had influence up, down, left, and right from wherever I was. That wasn't always the case for the formal leaders.

One memorable example is the time I was on the plant floor leading a kazien team when the area supervisor brought an issue to my attention. The kaizen team was working in his area of responsibility to help improve the department's processes. He was the process owner, and therefore involved, although he wasn't formally on the team as some of his associates were.

This supervisor wasn't really bought-in. Like anyone who wasn't bought-in would be, he was resistant to the changes we were making.

He approached me complaining about how some parts were now being stacked on the pallets and wanted me to fix it. He blamed the department who handled the parts just before they came to his area for stacking the parts the wrong way and slowing down the work in his area.

He proceeded to tell me if the team in the other department would simply flip them over when they loaded the pallets, it would make things much easier. He said they could just as easily stack them either way. I asked which department was supplying the parts. He turned and pointed to a department less than 50 yards away. I thought to myself, *"You've got to be kidding!"*

I asked him why he hadn't already asked them to make the change. He replied, *"They won't do what I tell them. They don't report to me."* I've seen and heard the same story countless times. No relationship. No influence. No leadership. No ownership. No culture of kaizen.

I said, *"Walk with me. Let's see if we can make it happen right now."* I already knew the supervisor and the team in the other department because I had been leading kaizen events in their area too. I had a relationship with them. I walked up to the supervisor, called him by name, shook his hand with a smile, and gave him a pat on the back.

I said, *"Did you know if your team will flip the parts over when stacking it will help the next operation unload them?"* He said, *"No I didn't, but we'll make the change immediately."* And, he did. Mission accomplished in less than one minute.

Why did I have to make that happen? Why couldn't the supervisor with the issue make it happen? Why wouldn't he talk to his peer? Because they didn't have a relationship. They were focused on doing their job (competency), not on building relationships (character).

Character and competency create authentic influence. Research has shown that 87% of our influence comes from our character (who we are) and only 13% of our influence comes from our competency (what we know).

Authentic influence trumps positional authority every time.

To create a kaizen culture, you must focus on developing your own character and then helping others develop theirs. At a minimum, intentionally grow and develop the character of those on the teams you lead.

Leadership development is character development. Leadership is influence. Everyone has influence. Therefore, everyone can lead (influence) others positively or negatively. High impact Lean leaders intentionally model and teach character-based leadership principles.

"Character isn't something you were born with and can't change, like your fingerprints. It's something you weren't born with and must take responsibility for forming." ~ Jim Rohn

5

MAKE IT HAPPEN!

MANAGERS MAKE A PLAN;
HIGH IMPACT LEADERS MAKE IT HAPPEN

"In any moment of decision, the best thing you can do is the right thing, the next best thing is the wrong thing, and the worst thing you can do is nothing."
~ Theodore Roosevelt

I had been leading Lean/kaizen events for three years before I started studying and reading leadership. In the beginning, I didn't realize how important it was to learn and apply leadership principles to get better results. All I had heard about were the Lean tools.

Nothing I read discussed having respect for the people in a way that really taught me how to respect the people. That's because most Lean experts are not leadership experts. They may be naturally good leaders, but most haven't actually studied, applied, and taught leadership development formally for many years as I now have.

I've read hundreds of leadership development books and written 11 of my own, including two others in the *Blue-Collar Leadership Series*. I learned to apply leadership principles while leading Lean transformations and kaizen events. As a result, I'm uniquely qualified to provide you with insight that few Lean experts can.

As a high impact Lean leader, you're responsible for making things happen. I'm packing this little book full of stories and principles in an effort to motivate and inspire you to intentionally embrace personal growth and leadership development on an entirely new level.

Consider the statistics I mentioned. 87% of your influence (results) comes from character, and 13% from competency. In Lean language, that means 87% of your influence is based on Respect for the People, and 13% is based on Continuous Improvement. Character multiplies competency. You can leverage the Lean tools and multiply their effectiveness by Respecting the People.

In the last chapter, I shared an example of how my relationships with kaizen team members helped me make things happen. Now, I'm going to share a story of how developing my character allowed me to make things happen. The key for me was developing self-control.

Self-control is always the right thing. As Theodore Roosevelt said, *"The best thing you can do is the right thing…"*

In 2009, I toured a facility with a new client to identify a pilot area for their first kaizen event. Walking through the plant, the plant manager and I discussed the possibilities of the pilot area. I reminded him these were only possibilities and asked him not to discuss them, as we couldn't be sure what the team would decide to do.

I returned a few weeks later for the event. We had only five days to make things happen. On day one, the team members met me for the first time. I was glad one of the team members was the operator from the area we were going to focus on. Having him involved would be critical to the success of the event.

I asked the operator, as I always do, *"Last week, what were you thinking about this week?"*

He angrily replied, *"I couldn't wait until you got here, so I could cut your damn throat!"*

I was shocked. I didn't know this man. This man didn't know me.

However, I knew *nothing* was going to happen until we got past his intense anger toward me. The right response was critical. I tried to ease the tension in the room with, *"Why don't you tell us how you really feel sir?"*

My reply didn't soften his anger, but it did let him know I didn't take it personally, and we could talk about it. He was angry. I knew losing my self-control wasn't going to increase my influence with him or anyone else, and it wouldn't solve the issue. You won't be a high impact Lean leader if you can't control yourself when others don't.

After a few questions, I discovered the root cause of his anger was hearing a rumor his area was going to be changed and his work platform, among other things, would be removed.

Avoiding rumors like this was the reason I had asked the plant manager not to share the possibilities we discussed. He hadn't listened.

I assured the operator he was the most important part of our team, and while the team would recommend changes, he had the final say. I also told him if he wanted the platform to stay and it was removed anyway, I would leave and not return. I won't work with leaders who don't respect their people. I built trust with him. By Wednesday, the operator was on a fork lift tossing his platform in the scrap bin out back.

I didn't always have that level of self-control. I gained it by learning how to lead myself well through studying and applying leadership principles. High impact Lean leaders make it happen because of their character.

"Some men have thousands of reasons why they cannot do what they want to, when all they need is one reason why they can." ~ Willis R. Whitney

6

LEADING UP

RESULTS INCREASE INFLUENCE ABOVE

"Greatness is not a function of circumstance. Greatness, it turns out, is largely a matter of conscious choice, and discipline." ~ Jim Collins

Discipline is a choice. Self-control is a choice. Personal development is a choice. Doing more than required is a choice. Doing things before they are required is a choice. Doing things better than required is a choice. Intentionally developing your character is a choice.

Accepting responsibility for getting results regardless of the situation or circumstance is a choice. When it comes to building trust and gaining influence with the leaders who are formally responsible for moving the organization forward, the quickest way to do it is to get results as defined by them, not you.

As a high impact Lean leader, your mission is to get results in a way that demonstrates respect to all of the people involved, even those who may want to *"cut your throat."* And yes, to achieve success, you must get results for those weak, insecure low impact leaders who undermine you on a regular basis. That's the reality of the world. They exist. The best leaders find a way to make it happen regardless of their circumstances.

I remember starting a new consulting contract with an organization many years ago. They had previously worked with another consultant but had only focused on 5S. I was glad because I would get to focus on the Lean tools I liked the most Quick ChangeOver (SMED/QCO) for reducing changeover time and Standard Work for increasing productivity. We also conducted Total Productive Maintenance (TPM), Value Stream Mapping (VSM), Production Preparation Process (3P), and additional 5S events too.

I was brought in for a few days before I officially started leading kaizen events to learn about the operations. On day two, I was asked to meet with the plant manager. He informed me they were in crisis mode with a new product at a facility I hadn't visited yet. He wanted to know if I could and would help.

I knew I could help because I unleash people's potential. I don't need to know all the answers. As long as I have questions, the team will provide the answers.

I make things happen with people who want to make things happen. I knew I had his support. I also knew this was the perfect opportunity to get results, very important results, from the very start by leading my first event in a critical area. I didn't know anything about the process, but I knew I could help them do it better and more efficiently.

I told him I needed six to eight people on the team: at least one operator from the area, maintenance personnel, supervision, quality personnel, engineering personnel, someone in an administration role from outside the area, and someone from upper management. He made it happen, and now it was my turn.

We kicked off the event the following Monday morning with the team fully assembled. They didn't have any knowledge about Lean beyond 5S. So, they were learning on the job. I love this kind of challenge! Why? Because it reveals my ability to quickly build trust, build relationships, influence people, and get results. In other words, my leadership ability is revealed for the world to see. I love to lead, so I was in my zone.

I quickly found out the leader of the work area and a few others were not excited to be participating in the week long kaizen event. They wanted to be working. They were frustrated, had little patience, and didn't mind letting everyone know it. They didn't know me, but they did know I was there to help them do what they seemed unable to do: produce 120 of the new components per day.

I learned they had been working 10-12 hour days, seven days a week for several weeks in an effort to make it happen. They had been unsuccessful, were giving up, and were now looking at outsourcing as an option in order to deliver the product on time. They were producing 35 components per day with seven people working 10 hours. They didn't see how a stranger with no knowledge of what they were doing could help.

Fast forward. By Wednesday, the leader of the area came in and said he actually got some sleep because he could see where we were headed. By the end of the day on Friday, the entire area had been redesigned with a new layout. They were producing 120 components with five people in eight hours. The improvement based on the actual event data reflected a 376% increase in output per person per hour. The team got results!

If you want to influence those at the top, get the results they want. Find a way to make it happen.

> *"You can't build a reputation on what you are going to do." ~ Henry Ford*

7

DEVELOP YOURSELF

IT'S NOT ABOUT YOU,
BUT IT BEGINS WITH YOU

*"You can never become a leader without doing more
than you are paid for, and you cannot become
successful without developing leadership in
your chosen occupation." ~ Napoleon Hill*

As a high impact Lean leader, the one thing you should be doing that you're most likely not going to be paid to do is intentionally developing yourself in the area of personal growth and leadership development. It will launch you like a rocket if you make it a habit. I teach it only because I have lived it.

Three years into my Lean leadership journey, after having led a very successful Lean transformation, I resigned from nearly 20 years in the corporate world to start my own Lean Consulting business. I had discovered my passion for leading kaizen teams and converting traditional batch and queue operations into streamlined Lean operations. I had never read a leadership book.

During my transition from the corporate world to starting my own business, I discovered professional leadership development. I had worked my way up from the front lines to become the Lean Manager at the plant level reporting directly to the plant manager. Not once during my entire corporate career had I received any formal leadership development training. I simply did a great job and got promoted to the next level which seems to be how it usually works in the blue-collar world.

This is the primary reason I have written this book for you. I want to do my part to expose as many Lean leaders to leadership development and personal growth as possible. When I discovered professional leadership content, I knew it was the missing Lean link.

I knew there was an entire world of content already focused on respect for the people. It didn't have to be invented. It was already there waiting for those of us in the Lean world to start soaking it up. However, because most Lean leaders are reading and studying Lean books, they are also focused only on the Lean tools.

They don't know what they don't know. Their lack of awareness is holding them and their teams back. During the three year Lean transformation I started in 2005 while I was reporting to Jim Noreault, we didn't have a formal leadership development program. We were simply all doing the best we could based on what we knew to do.

I didn't know what I know now. When you formally include personal growth and leadership development as part of your Lean program as a way to demonstrate respect for the people, you are playing on a level far beyond most Lean organizations.

However, you must first develop yourself, so you can develop others. You must become intentional and start reading leadership books, listening to leadership audios, and watching leadership videos. It doesn't matter which you prefer, but it will matter if you don't do any of them.

Leadership principles are timeless and tested. They apply in all areas, in all industries, and with all people. Many people learn practices that will work in only one situation. You should be learning principles that will always work in all situations.

For example, relative to Lean, many people across many industries say, *"Lean won't work here. What Toyota did worked for them, but it won't work for us."* Anyone who makes that comment is talking about the practice, or what they can see on the surface. The practice they see may not work in their operations. However, the underlying principle Toyota applied to achieve their results will apply in every operation in any location.

I always recommend reading at least one paragraph per day, every day, from a leadership book. If you want to read more that's great, but you must still have the discipline to read at least one paragraph tomorrow, regardless of how much you read today. Reading leadership is an investment in yourself. It's like investing money in the bank. It compounds over time.

As of mid-2017, my wife, Ria, and I have published 19 books. If you like this book, be sure to check out our others. Do your own research and start reading from authors who interest you. Don't worry if they aren't Lean experts. You're looking for leadership experts.

Unleash your potential by becoming intentional.

"Nothing is given to man on earth except a potential and the material on which to actualize it. The potential is a superlative machine: his consciousness; but it is a machine without a spark plug, a machine of which his own will has to be the spark plug, the self-starter and the driver; he has to discover how to use it and he has to keep it in constant action. The material is the whole of the universe, with no limits set to the knowledge he can acquire and to the enjoyment of life he can achieve. But everything he needs or desires has to be learned, discovered and produced by him — by his own choice, by his own effort, by his own mind."
~ Ayn Rand

BlueCollarLeaders.com

8

DEVELOP OTHERS

THE BEST LEADERS GO SLOW TO GO FAST

"Lean managers go slow to go fast, by taking the time at the outset to fully understand the process and its purpose, through dialogue with everyone involved...and by fully understanding the root cause of problems and the most promising counter-measure before taking action." ~ Jim Womack

In companies struggling to get buy-in to Lean and/or struggling to sustain the gain, the underlying root cause is a lack of respect for the people. Most companies think respect for the people means allowing them to participate on a Lean team, giving them a turkey at Thanksgiving, and providing a cost of living raise when they can.

These types of practices have very little to do with respect for the people. They have a lot to do with trying to keep their associates from quitting and going to work for the competition. The best companies do more than is required to demonstrate respect for the people. The best companies are focused not only on intentionally improving the processes, but also on intentionally developing and respecting their people.

I've told my audiences when speaking, *"If I was responsible for leading an organization through a Lean transformation and I had to choose between focusing on respect for the people or continuous improvement, I wouldn't have to think about it. I would choose to focus my efforts on respect for the people."*

22

When leaders focus on growing and developing the people for the right reasons, the people feel it. As a result, they do what they can to show their appreciation. They become more productive, improve processes, improve quality, share more ideas, and speak highly of the company and its leaders in public. In other words, they start living kaizen and spreading positive word of mouth advertisement for the company.

When most companies start down the Lean path, they get it wrong. They don't follow Womack's advice. They don't *"go slow to go fast."* They do just the opposite. They *go fast to go slow*. They are hungry for the results they have read about in the Lean books and on the consultant's website. Instead of doing Lean with the people, they do Lean to the people. And, the people feel it.

What's the result? Resistance. Sometimes, it's extreme resistance such as, *"I want to cut your throat!"*

Most often, it's passive resistance. Because the leaders don't know what they don't know about leadership, they don't even call it resistance. They simply think that's the way it is. What does passive resistance look like? It looks like people participating during the Lean events, but not sustaining the gains afterwards. Why? Because they don't have to, and they don't want to.

People follow low impact leaders because they have to. While on the job, these same people usually only do what they have to do to keep their job. Since they don't usually have to sustain the gains to keep their job, they don't.

People follow high impact leaders because they want to. While on the job, these people do much more than is required. They not only sustain the gains, but they also offer suggestions and make improvements to create additional gains. They are living kaizen because they respect their leaders and want to help them succeed.

In 2009, I began formally introducing my Lean clients to leadership development and personal growth. I included it as part of the respect for the people component and used the standard Lean tools to support the continuous improvement component.

If you're going to excel at the highest level as a high impact Lean leader, you must do more than master and teach the Lean tools. That's only half of the equation. You must also accept responsibility for growing and developing the people.

I offer my clients a 5-day Lean Leadership Certification Course. Organizations with high impact leaders see the value in taking all of their associates through this training before they are asked to participate on any kaizen events. The week consists of 80% personal growth and leadership development and 20% covering the basics about the Lean tools and their application.

Everyone is included. Even the outside sales team members from around the country. I mix up the teams with members from different departments, areas, and even different levels of the organization. A typical team may have welders, directors, engineers, operators, and material handlers. The more diverse, the better, because diversity improves teamwork and communication across the organization.

Respect for the people is going slow to go fast. When you respect the people, you will prepare and equip them.

"Standards of excellence are not chiseled in stone. They are constantly being redefined. It's important to recognize that what was graded as excellent last year may not be so this year. That is why we must keep mastering new skills." ~ Bobb Beihl

9

RIGHTING THE WRONG

LEAN IS NOT ABOUT TWO PILLARS; IT'S ABOUT TWO FOUNDATIONAL LAYERS

"Being intentional about discovering the hidden ways in which we sabotage ourselves empowers us to expose and eliminate these invisible culprits."
~ Amir Ghannad

I'm not sure who actually developed the concept of Lean consisting of two pillars: continuous improvement and respect for the people. What I do know is all the Lean books I've read teach the two pillar model.

I actually taught the two pillar Lean model for years as many Lean leaders still do today. However, as I've grown and developed a deeper understanding of the people side of Lean, I've come to disagree with the two pillar Lean model because it suggests the pillars are equal.

The pillars are not equal. Without authentic respect for the people, organizations cannot create, much less sustain, a culture of kaizen. They are simply traditional organizations with better tools and methods for improving their processes. But, they are not true Lean organizations with authentic respect for the people.

I'm reminded of one of my favorite quotes. Alvin Toffer had this to say, *"The illiterate of the 21st century will not be those who cannot read and write, but those who cannot learn, unlearn, and relearn."* I love this quote because it underscores the mindset of the successful Lean thinker.

It's the perfect quote to support the principle of continuous improvement.

My challenge to you at this moment is to consider the Lean model as two foundational layers instead of two traditional pillars.

The first layer is respect for the people which supports the second layer, continuous improvement.

I use the 87/13 principle to explain it.

The Lean foundation has the respect for the people layer at the base. The respect for the people layer makes up 87% of the Lean foundation. It's not only the thickest layer, but it's also the strongest and most important. It's the foundational layer that supports everything else.

The second layer is the continuous improvement layer which makes up 13% of the Lean foundation. This layer is where all of the traditional Lean tools and methodologies are found. They are important to Lean success too. However, it's the people who must choose to leverage these tools and methodologies for maximum benefit. With respect, they will. Without it, they won't.

The degree to which the people are respected will determine the degree to which they buy-in to continuous improvement efforts. Just as leaders do not have to authentically respect the people, the people do not have to authentically buy-in to the Lean initiatives and/or their leaders.

Influence is based on character (87%) and competency (13%). The character of the leaders will determine how well they lead and how much the people are respected. The competency of the leaders will determine how well they can manage the things and processes they are responsible for. You *should* lead people, but you *must* manage things and processes.

Many leaders in blue-collar organizations only focus

their efforts on developing the competency of their people. They provide the necessary training and development needed to perform the job related tasks, but not leadership development. Some may be high impact managers, but few are high impact leaders.

Relative to Lean leaders, the organizational leaders are focused on growing and developing the competency of the Lean leaders, but not their character. The leaders want their Lean leaders to teach the Lean tools in an effort to implement continuous improvement.

Unfortunately, many organizational leaders have no interest in developing their people. However, it's not personal. They also most often have no interest in developing themselves.

Low impact leaders don't want to develop the people. They want to use the people. No matter how many times the leaders say, *"Lean is all about the people."* It won't change how the people feel when they know they are being used.

As a high impact Lean leader, you are not only responsible for leading the continuous improvement efforts. You are also responsible for growing your influence in an effort to grow and develop the character of all leaders at all levels. To lead, you must lead.

The only way to intentionally grow the leaders is to first intentionally grow yourself. The greater the character of the leaders, the greater the respect for the people.

"The business of business is people.
Yesterday, today, and forever." ~ *Herb Kelleher*

10

CONTINUOUS IMPROVEMENT

LEADING YOURSELF AND OTHERS THROUGH CHANGE

"The great thing about business is that despite all the history, all the deeply embedded traditional dysfunctional management practices, and all the baggage of unhealthy relationships and corrosive cultures, it is possible at any moment in time to push the reset button, to embrace a different way of being, and experience dramatic change." ~ Bob Chapman

Look in the mirror. When it comes to your development, where has your focus been? Character or competency? Respect for the people? Or, continuous improvement? Learning about leadership or learning about the Lean tools?

Have you made leadership development and personal growth the foundation of your own personal journey? Have you accepted and embraced the responsibility for growing the character of the leaders in your organization? Or, have you done what many Lean leaders do: focus on the easy stuff, learning and teaching the Lean tools?

Do you need to do as Bob suggested and, *"push the reset button to embrace a different way of being and experience dramatic change?"* As a high impact Lean leader, your mission is to constantly push the reset button, not only on the processes you're trying to improve, but also on the minds you're trying to constantly develop.

I'm sure you're already well aware of the difficulty of trying to execute a mission with a team when people are not bought-in to the mission or their leaders. Resistance is always high and idea sharing is always low. It's impossible to get people to change when they don't want to change. If you want to change your ability to motivate and inspire others to embrace, accept, and lead change, you must first change your own mind.

My mission in this book is to help you unleash your own high impact leadership potential, so you can unleash the potential within others. I'm doing on these pages what you must do with those on the teams you are leading. You must get them to buy-in to you first, just as I'm trying to get you to buy-in to me.

People must buy-in to the leader before they will buy-in to the leader's vision. When you are leading a team, you are positioned to become their leader. However, unless they choose to follow you, you are not their leader.

I learned many years ago my team members are not going to buy-in to the low impact leaders in their organization, the ones who often assigned them to my team. But, I could get them to buy-in to me and each other during our time together. Once I learned how to create the right environment on every team I led, everything changed for the better. Because I was continuously improving myself, I learned to lead myself and others effectively through change.

In this chapter on continuous improvement, I'm not focused on improvement of the processes. I'm focused on improvement of the people, and I'm starting with you. Continuous improvement is a principle for growth and forward movement. It not only applies to processes which can be changed to improve the results, but it can also be applied to people to improve their results.

You are on a mission to motivate and inspire your team. That's what high impact Lean leaders do.

Those who aren't developing themselves and others are simply "puppets" for the low impact leaders within the organization who are trying to manipulate the people into making the leaders look good. It's about the leader's results. It's not respect for the people.

If this is happening, the people already know it. No one has to tell them. They can feel it. If this is happening in your organization, you are not in a Lean organization. You are in a traditional organization using Lean tools to manipulate the people. You can still become a high impact Lean leader, but you must swim against the current. People can respect you without respecting the organization's leaders.

High impact Lean leaders are not puppets. They lead themselves well and lead others with character and integrity regardless of their environment. I have led Lean teams and achieved amazing results while inside organizations with poor leadership at all levels.

For me, that was the norm, not the exception. Traditional organizations are traditional because they lack high impact leadership. I was brought in to reduce costs and increase profits, not to develop the people. However, I still developed the people.

When I walk into the room respecting the people, they feel it. It is real. It is authentic. Who their leaders are on the inside doesn't affect me. When I lead teams, I get results, increase profits, and reduce costs. But, I demonstrate respect for the people while doing it. High impact Lean leaders always do both.

"It's wonderful how much may be done if we are always doing!" ~ *Thomas Jefferson*

11

RESPECT FOR THE PEOPLE

LEADERS WHO RESPECT THE PEOPLE DEVELOP THE PEOPLE

"Treat a man as he appears to be and you make him worse. But treat a man as if he already were what he potentially could be, and you make him what he should be." ~ *Johann Wolfgang von Goethe*

I remember reading a sign as a teenager with the following words, *"If the truth hurts, it probably should."*

If your organization doesn't have a formal, ongoing leadership development program in place where everyone from the top leader to the entry-level team members receive training in the areas of leadership, communication, character development, time management, change management, and personal growth, your organization does not have respect for the people.

Organizations that respect the people always intentionally help develop the character of their people. Unfortunately, the vast majority of organizations do nothing when it comes to developing the people. And, they must live with the results of having an under-developed workforce: high turnover and low engagement.

A few years ago, I met with the owner of a company. He asked me to meet with him privately in his office to discuss an issue he was dealing with. He was struggling with letting a good associate go. In other words, he was about to fire someone who was actually doing a good job.

After listening to him explain the situation, I knew the problem wasn't related to the associate's competency but rather his character. Once the owner felt I understood the situation, he asked me what I thought.

To help him identify the root cause, I went to the whiteboard in his office and drew a large T in the center. I labeled the left side of the T as "Character 87%" and the right side of the T as "Competency 13%"

Then, I asked him to grade the troubled associate on a scale of 1-100 on competency. He said, *"I'll give him an 85. He's pretty sharp. His competency is not the problem."* Then, I asked him to score him on his character. He said, *"That's where the problem is. I'll give him a 20 on his character."*

My next question was, *"During your many years in this company, why have people been fired most often? Character or competency?"* Without giving it much thought, he said, *"That's easy. It's always character. If people want to learn, we can teach them to do the job. Doing the job is not an issue. Character is always the root cause of all issues."*

Next, I asked him to consider where he invested his training resources (time and money). I asked him to score himself in each area as he had done his troubled associate. He said, *"Competency is where we invest the most. Until we brought you in last year, we invested 100% of our resources on competency development. Relative to developing our people, I'll give myself a score of 95 on competency development and a score of 10 on character development."* As he was telling me his answer, I could see him having the "Aha!" moment internally.

Then, I did some simple math to illustrate what he was already beginning to see. Relative to the scores he gave his troubled associate, I computed .87 X 20 = 17.4 and .13 X 85 = 11.05. The total failing score was 28.45 out of 100. No wonder he was about to be fired.

Next, relative to how the development resources were

invested, I computed .87 X 10 = 8.7 and .13 X 95 = 12.35. The total failing score was 21.05 out of 100.

It's easy to see both the associate and the organization were failing each other. It's also easy to see why. Neither were focusing on character development.

You can easily validate this principle for yourself. In your career, I'm sure you have noticed people are most often hired for what they know (competency), but they are most often fired for who they are (character).

As a high impact Lean leader, you must grow yourself and then leverage your influence in order to make character development a priority throughout your organization. Respecting the people is developing the people. Turnover, lack of engagement, lack of buy-in, finger-pointing, bad-mouthing, resistance, and lack of communication are signs of weak character among the leaders and their associates.

High impact Lean leaders know what I know. At a minimum, they intentionally incorporate a character development component into every Lean event.

"We make some of the best industrial machinery in the world. But, I will not go to my grave being proud of all the machines we have built. Instead, I will be deeply grateful for all the lives that we touched and uplifted in our journey. The machinery we build is just the economic engine that enables us to touch lives. The flourishing of those lives is our paramount concern."
~ Bob Chapman

12

THE EMOTIONAL TRUST ACCOUNT

YOU ARE EITHER MAKING
DEPOSITS OR WITHDRAWALS

"If I try to use human influence strategies and tactics of how to get other people to do what I want, to work better, to be more motivated, to like me and each other - while my character is fundamentally flawed, marked by duplicity or insincerity - then, in the long run, I cannot be successful. My duplicity will breed distrust, and everything I do - even using so-called good human relations techniques - will be perceived as manipulative." ~ Dr. Stephen R. Covey

In order to become a high impact Lean leader, you must develop 360° of influence. Your influence will become critical when you're leading kaizen teams because you will need a lot of help and support if you and the team are going to make some really great things happen.

Influence is absolutely critical for Lean leaders because they are trying to influence team members to follow and help them, even when they don't have to. You can intentionally increase your influence with anyone if you apply the appropriate leadership principles. Once you learn to increase your influence, you will be in a position to teach the underlying principles to those on your teams.

Trust is the foundation of authentic influence. Without trust, you will only have influence over people who have to follow you. As you and I both know, kaizen team members do not have to follow us. Yet, we are responsible for delivering results. Leadership is about accepting, rather than avoiding, responsibility.

If you aren't willing to accept responsibility for your results, you are not a high impact Lean leader. You are a low impact Lean leader creating distrust and losing influence across the organization.

The key to getting great results with a team is to build trust as quickly as possible. If you do the things you're learning in this book, you will begin building stronger relationships with many people who will trust you and want to help you.

Sometimes, it's possible to build great relationships with people before they participate on one of your kaizen teams. That's a tremendous opportunity and you should take advantage of it.

Imagine doing what I did week after week, year after year. I would show up on Monday to lead a team of people I usually didn't know. If I couldn't build trust quickly in those situations, I would be doomed from the start.

To build trust quickly, it helps to know what the emotional trust account is and how it works. The emotional trust account works much like a bank account. You make deposits, withdrawals, and occasionally, there will be automatic withdrawals.

Emotional trust accounts are opened automatically between you and every individual you come in contact with and everyone who hears something good or bad about you. If you want to increase your influence, you must make intentional deposits. Otherwise, you'll become overdrawn.

Instead of depositing or withdrawing money, you are making deposits into the emotional trust accounts with other people when you do something to build trust. You are making withdrawals when you do something to create distrust. You may also do something unintentionally and unknowingly that creates distrust. These are referred to as automatic withdrawals. They happen all the time. You must be making deposits to offset the them.

As a Lean leader, you will often start a kaizen event overdrawn, especially if there is little or no respect for the people in the organization. Team members may start the event already distrusting you, distrusting the leadership of the organization, and resistant to change. They don't have to be told if there is or isn't respect for the people. They already know. Based on their feelings, there will be trust or distrust.

For years, this was how I started each event each week. My emotional trust accounts with most people were overdrawn when I met them. Weak leaders in the organization had made withdrawals for me, and other consultants before me had made withdrawals for me. Based on the stories the team members had told themselves about me, I was already overdrawn without speaking a word to them.

However, I was always able to overcome the distrust by intentionally building trust. If you're going to get meaningful results, you must build trust with the people on the team as quickly as possible.

All team members want to know three things for sure: 1) Can I trust you? 2) Will you help me? 3) Do you respect me?

Imagine you are on my team next Monday morning. How could I build trust? How could I create distrust?

"Trust is the one thing that changes everything."
~ Stephen M. R. Covey

13

DECLARE YOUR INTENT

HELP THE TEAM SEE
AND FEEL THE RIGHT THINGS

"Followers choose to follow a leader with a compelling purpose, vision, cause, or goal, the unifying purpose. It is the leader's unifying purpose that attracts the interest and loyalty of followers. The leader is someone who is able to communicate unifying purpose in a manner that is inspiring, persuasive, or motivating. The unifying purpose joins the followers to the leader." ~ Jimmy Collins

When I started leading Lean teams, I was fired up and excited to improve the processes. I wanted to prove I could make a difference. I loved the challenge of improving processes. However, I no longer work in the area of process improvement. Today, my only focus is on developing the people, especially those people who lead other people through change.

As I got started, I quickly learned not everyone shares my enthusiasm about process improvement. Not everyone likes being in the spotlight. Not everyone likes working together as a team. Not everyone likes their job. Not everyone likes their boss. Not everyone likes me.

I learned what builds trust with one person may create distrust with another person. If you've never really thought about it, we trust those who are like us and who value what we value. Different people have different values. The one thing everyone values is themselves.

As a result, the quickest way to build trust is to make the team members feel valued. You can do this immediately by declaring your intent as soon as you kick-off the kaizen event with your team. Declare you are leading, but you are also a team member. Declare you don't want credit and will give them all the credit for the team's success. Declare you want to help them help themselves by making things better not worse.

What does "declare your intent" mean? It means you tell the team what to look for, so they see the right thing in the right way. Tell them why you're about to do or say something before you do or say it. By doing so, you are aligning their thinking with your intention. Otherwise, they will tell themselves a story about your behavior, words, and actions. Often, their story is not in alignment with reality.

Here's an example of declaring intent. I often talk about my past successes with other teams at the start of an event with new teams. I declar my intent before I start telling the related stories. I say something like, *"I'm about to share some past successes with you. I'm doing this, so you can see I've had success in the past with teams just like you in similar situations. I'm not doing it to impress you, but to inspire you because you can achieve the same amazing results. I'll also be sharing ideas I've learned from others to provoke new thoughts and new ideas you may not have considered."*

Declaring your intent means you insure the team is telling themselves an accurate story. There's one thing you need to know: No one believes anything you say. They only believe what they tell themselves about what you say. You likely just did it to me and have been doing it throughout this book. We do it all the time consciously and subconsciously without really thinking about it.

If you tell yourself you agree, you believe me. If you tell yourself you disagree, you don't believe me. However, your belief is based on the story you told yourself about what I said. It's not actually based on what I said. You need to know this because this is what's happening when you're talking to members of the teams you lead.

When you're leading a kaizen event, your words and actions must be aligned. If they are aligned, people will tell themselves a story that builds trust. If they are not aligned, people will tell themselves a story that creates distrust. I'm sure you already know they will also tell each other stories about you too. Trust increases your influence. Distrust decreases your influence.

When it comes to leading Lean, who you are matters much more than what you know. If you focus on the Lean tools and improving the processes, but you're not learning and applying leadership principles, you're in for a struggle.

When it comes to intent, you are either manipulating or motivating. When your intent is to manipulate, it's not about me. Only you benefit. I don't. When your intent is to motivate, it's all about "we." Everyone benefits.

Declaring intent provides a clear vision in advance about why you're doing what you're doing. In the end, people value and trust people who value and trust them.

"Leaders do not have to be the greatest visionaries themselves. The vision may come from anyone. The leaders do have to state the vision, however. Leaders also have to keep the vision before the people and remind them of the progress that is being made to achieve the vision. Otherwise, the people might assume that they are failing and give up."
~ Ezra Earl Jones

14

CONNECT FIRST

COMMUNICATION IS ABOUT INFORMATION; CONNECTION IS ABOUT INSPIRATION

"A great man is always willing to be little."
~ Ralph Waldo Emerson

High impact Lean leaders are willing to be humble. They kick off team events by making it about the team, not about themselves or the process. The go slow to go fast. They focus on relationships before they focus on results. They take time to get to know team members at the start of an event. They ask lots of questions, so they and other team members can learn about each other. They want to know who the team members are, not just what they do.

Low impact Lean leaders aren't willing to be humble. They start off team events with pride, ego, and arrogance. They treat team members as objects to be used to improve the process, not people to be valued and helped. They often say or do things that make team members feel uncomfortable. They often give short answers. Sometimes, they give no answers at all. They don't try to connect because they prefer to direct.

There's a fine line between arrogance and confidence. It's called humility. High impact Lean leaders stay humble, so they don't stumble.

Low impact Lean leaders don't try to communicate.

Average Lean leaders try to communicate. However, high impact Lean leaders not only communicate well, but they also connect with others intentionally. As my wife, Ria, says, *"Connection multiplies communication."* High impact Lean leaders are always multipliers. They leverage communication with connection.

When we communicate, we are interacting with the conscious mind of others. As a result, we *may* be able to change what they do or don't do from the outside with our words. Communication is about motivation. Motivation comes from the outside.

When we connect, we are interacting with the subconscious mind of others. As a result, we are able to change how they think and feel on the inside. Connection is about inspiration. Inspiration comes from the inside.

Anyone can communicate. All you must do is have information and be willing to share that information. When you share information, you are officially communicating. You may or may not be building trust.

Few people can connect. Connecting has less to do with information and more to do with creating positive feelings. When you are connecting with another person, you are always building trust. High impact Lean leaders intentionally learn how to connect. Then, they do it relentlessly every day whether they are leading a team or simply interacting with others throughout their day.

I've trained a lot of Lean leaders. I've also supported a lot of leaders who volunteered to lead a kaizen event or who were "voluntold" to lead a kaizen event.

Those who volunteered were much more fun to work with. At least, they had some interest. It was easy to get them to buy-in. Those who were "voluntold" were not so much fun to work with. They had very little, if any, interest. It was difficult at best to get them to buy-in, and impossible at worst.

People who do not want to lead an event are not interested in communicating, much less connecting. They should not be pressured into leading an event.

One way to demonstrate respect for the people is by not pressuring others into leading teams. Instead, find someone who wants to lead a team, lead it yourself, or cancel the event. But, don't do what low impact leaders do; don't use authority to pressure someone into leading an event.

High impact leaders would never pressure someone into leading a kaizen event because it would be disrespectful to the individual, the team, the Lean process, and to those who are watching. It also sends a very clear message: We do not respect the people.

High impact leaders know the value of connecting. As a result, they build strong relationships and develop those who show an interest in leading events. They invest time with them on the front end. They build their confidence. They teach them what's in this book and many others while providing the necessary training and support in advance to help them succeed. In other words, they move beyond communicating and start connecting.

You do not connect with people by pressuring them to do things they don't want to do. You can't connect with people by ignoring them and not listening to them. You connect with people by listening to them. Listen and learn. When you do, you will increase your influence.

"Taking the conversation away from another person is a common form of lack of self-control which is not only discourteous, but it deprives those who do it of many valuable opportunities to learn from others."
~ Napoleon Hill

15

WASTE DOESN'T MOTIVATE

ELIMINATING FRUSTRATIONS
GETS EVERYONE MOTIVATED

"Lean is not really about waste elimination, it's about frustration elimination, removing obstacles that stand in the way of people being their best, that prevent us from having a joyful and meaningful experience. It's not about telling, it's about listening. It's about blending unique knowledge with collective wisdom. When we allow people and their teams to own the process, they can create better outcomes than any senior executive or group of consultants."
~ Bob Chapman

"Eliminating waste" is probably the most commonly used Lean phrase. However, nobody gets too excited about eliminating wastes, except maybe those in accounting because they naturally see dollars being saved. The thought of eliminating waste doesn't spark passion in many people. To begin with, most have to be taught what waste is relative to Lean.

Few people wake up on a Monday morning excited to join a kaizen event to "eliminate waste." But, if you change the goal to "eliminate frustrations," they don't need training to understand. People easily get excited about getting rid of their frustrations and naturally buy-in. Eliminating frustrations, roadblocks, and problems in everyday work is something everyone can relate to.

43

If you want to accelerate buy-in, stop talking about eliminating wastes and start talking about eliminating frustrations. When it comes to influence, words matter.

The sooner you get buy-in, the sooner you can leverage the knowledge, skills, and abilities of those who can help you move the organization forward.

If you want to communicate to your team, talk about eliminating wastes. If you want to connect with your team, talk about eliminating frustrations. It's common sense, but it's not common practice.

When I read Bob Chapman's thoughts about focusing on eliminating frustrations instead of eliminating wastes in his book, *Everybody Matters: The Extraordinary Power of Caring for Your People Like Family*, my first thought was, *"Why didn't I think of that?"* When you read his words, think about them, and reflect on them, it's easy to understand the common sense thought process Bob utilized to develop his insight.

Words matter, and they matter a lot. I wish I had known to say these words and understood the impact they would have on my ability to motivate, inspire, and influence others from the very start because it would have tremendously accelerated my ability to gain buy-in to my Lean mission. But, I was learning, as I still am, with every book I read.

Imagine you're on my kaizen team next Monday morning as we start to tackle another area that has been targeted for improvement. Imagine you are the operator from the targeted area. Imagine you know very little about Lean. Imagine you've heard a lot of negative talk about Lean and maybe even me since I'm the one leading Lean. Imagine you don't know what to expect.

I want to illustrate the power words have on your ability to influence and create buy-in quickly using two different, yet very simple, and impactful scenarios.

Scenario #1: Everyone is assembled for an 8am kick-off. At 8am, I walk to the front of the room and say, *"I'm ready to eliminate wastes this week. I hope you are too. Lean is about systematically identifying and eliminating wastes in any process. Waste elimination will be our primary focus this week. I'll teach you how. Then, we'll go make it happen. Let's get started."*

Scenario #2: Everyone is assembled for an 8am kick-off. At 8am, I walk to the front of the room and ask, *"Have any of you ever been frustrated while at work? I'd like to hear about it. (Then, I give everyone a chance to share some of their frustrations. And, they gladly will.) Kaizen is about coming together as a team to identify and eliminate your frustrations in an effort to make your work experience better. If you want an opportunity to eliminate frustrations, you're in the right place. Who thinks eliminating frustrations will make your job and your life better?"*

Based only on these two very brief, but very different opening statements, which would get your attention? Which would create a feeling of hope? Which would you be more likely to mention to your family after work? Which would gain more buy-in? Which would engage your mind? Which would cause you to start thinking about things that need to be improved?

Your words and your vision are powerful tools of influence. Leadership is influence. High impact Lean leaders have people who volunteer to follow them. High impact Lean leaders cast a vision, gain buy-in, and have followers who will help them execute the mission.

"Vision without execution is hallucination."
~ Thomas Edison

16

LISTEN TO THE VOICES

TAKE THE TIME IT TAKES,
SO IT TAKES LESS TIME

"Listening is the greatest communication tool to use when you want to connect with someone." ~ Ria Story

For several years, my biggest mistake when I started leading kaizen teams was doing all the talking. I started my kaizen events much like Scenario #1 in the last chapter.

I didn't just open that way. I led the team that way the entire week. I thought since I was the expert and had a lot of Lean knowledge, I should do most of the talking. I didn't know what I didn't know. But, I learned.

As time passed, I slowly began to get better at listening and letting the team do more of the talking. However, when I discovered and started reading leadership development books three years into my Lean journey, everything clicked. I quickly shifted my kaizen team leadership style to that reflected in Scenario #2.

Then, I learned what Dean Rusk meant when he said, *"One of the best ways to persuade others is with your ears - by listening to them."* I switched gears. I changed my style. I developed more *respect for the people*. I started asking more questions right from the start.

Initially, I thought asking questions of the team was slowing me down because I wasn't teaching and directing the team. But, I was okay with that because I knew I was connecting with them instead of communicating with them. At that point, connecting was more important to me than directing. I was willing to slow down to make a better connection.

After several months of focusing on connecting through questions, I realized I wasn't going slower. The teams were accomplishing more. They were actually going faster, not slower. They were buying-in quicker too.

I was no longer trying to get the teams to follow me down the Lean path. They began walking down the Lean path on their own. Instead of leading them down the path, I chose to travel alongside them as a team member.

When necessary, I would run ahead and remove obstacles. When necessary, I would get out of their way. When necessary, I would be the loudest cheerleader on the team. When necessary, I would connect the team with others who could help. When necessary, I would ask questions. When necessary, I would listen and learn.

When necessary, I listened to the voices. When necessary, leaders should stop leading and start following.

For example, I remember leading a team of 10-12 top leaders of a 600 person plant through a kaizen event. In blue-collar language, all the "big dogs" were in the room at one time in an effort to develop a plan to improve flow through a bottle neck operation that involved multiple departments and support groups such as inventory control, production planning, etc.

The lack of flow had plagued them and the organization for years. This wasn't their first attempt to improve it. They had tried many times in the past before I showed up on the scene. They hadn't made much progress. Now, I was there, and it was time to try again.

At that point in my kaizen team leading journey, I had learned to *take the time it takes, so it takes less time.* If I had not mastered this principle, that week would have been a disaster. But, I got it right. It was a huge success.

I knew from the start this would be a tough event. I had been working with these leaders for many months separately. I knew there was some finger-pointing and bad-mouthing going on in this group. Now, they had to sit in the same room and work together on their shared problem. It was obvious they didn't want to.

Within the first few hours on Monday morning, they were already telling themselves there was nothing they could do, they had tried everything already, and the event was a waste of time. They were not shining. They were whining. I kept asking questions and kept listening.

All they wanted to talk about was why everything everyone suggested wouldn't work or had already been tried unsuccessfully. I literally listened to this non-stop until mid-day Wednesday.

Then I said, *"If there's nothing you can do. Let's end it. I'll go home, and you guys can go back to work."* I asked someone to put the final presentation slides up on the screen and type, "There's nothing we can do." Then I asked, *"When do you want to present your results to the owner?"*

They said, *"We can't tell him that."* I asked, *"Well then, what can you do?"* I never forced it. I simply listened and learned. Everyone finally felt understood. As a result, they found a way to move forward together. Then, they did.

"We changed the name from 'Lean' to 'Living Legacy of Leadership' because in the early stages of embracing these powerful leadership ideas, it became clear to us that Lean as widely practiced was mostly about numbers and not about people. If the Toyota production processes had been studied and named properly, it would have been called Listen."
~ Bob Chapman

17

THE KEY TO BUY-IN

LEARN TO LEVERAGE THE MEETINGS BEFORE THE MEETING

"No man can persuade people to do what he wants them to do, unless he genuinely likes people, and believes that what he wants them to do is to their own advantage." ~ Bruce Barton

Far too many Lean leaders are getting mediocre results at best or poor results at worst because they don't know they should be having *the meetings before the meeting*. Or, they are unwilling to invest the time and energy to have *the meetings before the meeting*.

The principle I'm teaching can be applied to the meeting (kaizen event) or any other type of meeting where you need to gain buy-in from individuals and agreement from the group as a whole. Regardless of the type of meeting, the meetings before the meeting will always allow you to significantly increase your influence, not only before the meeting, but also during the meeting.

If you leverage the meetings before the meeting with mutual benefit in mind and work through concerns in advance, the actual meeting will be a stroll in the park. If you don't, it may be more like a climb up Mt. Everest.

I recommend taking the time it takes, so it takes less time overall. Be intentional. Plan. Connect. Make deposits. It will take more time and energy to connect than it will to communicate. Go slow to go fast.

A Lean leader can often schedule a kaizen event by email. Request team members from various department leaders by email. Wait for the event date to arrive. Then, kick-off the kaizen event without ever actually speaking to the leaders or the team members who were assigned to participate.

That's exactly how many Lean leaders put together a kaizen team. I've seen it done repeatedly. Why? People are busy, and it's the simplest and easiest way. But, it doesn't demonstrate respect for the people.

Where's the problem? The root cause of the lack of respect is the Lean leader's choice not to have the meetings before the meeting.

For example, I supported many Lean leaders with kaizen events as a consultant. They worked onsite and were on the ground doing all the work in advance to make the event happen. Then, I showed up on Monday morning to actually lead the event.

Far too many times, when the team members walk in the room on day one, they are already complaining because they just found out that morning they would be participating in the kaizen event all week long. This happens to people on the front lines, people in formal leadership positions at all levels, and everyone in between.

No one communicated with them in advance, much less made the attempt to connect with them. No one, including the Lean leader, made connecting a priority.

This happens all the time. It's totally disrespectful.

It's also a huge withdrawal for those who didn't get any notice and for those who are in the room witnessing to how the others have been disrespected by their leaders. I get blamed, the Lean leader gets blamed, and the leaders who didn't inform their team members get blamed.

Huge withdrawals are being made from multiple

emotional trust accounts all at the same time. Everyone on the team will pay the price because it is not only disrespectful, it is also disrupting. People are going to talk, and most will moan, groan, and whine. The worst part is all of it could have been avoided.

Getting amazing results consistently is not effortless. High impact Lean leaders invest a lot of time and energy preparing for an event before the event happens. They fully understand the importance of making deposits and avoiding withdrawals.

They don't simply gather a list of names for a kaizen event and show up on day one expecting to have great success. That's a recipe for a painful event. It may go okay, but odds are, it won't go as good as it could have gone. The meetings before the meeting will insure everyone is onboard with the Lean leader and ready to go.

High impact Lean leaders intentionally start building relationships and gaining buy-in well before the actual event (meeting) kicks off. How? They cast the vision, ask questions, and discuss concerns. They meet with the leaders. They meet with the team members. They meet with the process owners. They meet with the value stream managers. They meet with those who will support the event such as: inventory control, maintenance, engineering, safety, quality, etc. Then, when the event kicks off, they are ready to make things happen.

High impact Lean leaders are methodical and intentional about casting the vision, gaining buy-in, and creating an environment for success.

"The individual in your organization who communicates the clearest vision will often be perceived as the leader. Clarity is perceived as leadership." ~ Andy Stanley

18

BE A LEADER

PROCESSES AND THINGS DON'T THINK AND FEEL, BUT PEOPLE DO

"Managers change behavior. Leaders change the way you think without you realizing it." ~ Daniel Burrus

As a high impact Lean leader, you must understand the difference between managing and leading. You must learn the differences and how to apply the principles of each, so you can get great results and inspire others to do the same. You must also model the appropriate leader behavior and the appropriate manager behavior at the right times for the right reasons in order to give meaning to your words and your actions.

I often use the following example when trying to help people understand the difference between leadership and management. We must help others see the difference.

Assume for a moment, I'm a manager who just finished an all-day Lean class on how to improve productivity by creating single-piece flow and eliminating any batch and queue processes whenever possible. I had an "Aha!" moment in class and realized I had the perfect opportunity in my department.

The next day, I tell my team about the changes I'll be making. Then, I start directing them on what to do, what goes, what stays, and how I expect things to work.

The team will do as they are told to keep their job,

plus they already know this is how I operate. They most likely will bad-mouth me once I leave the area because that's how they operate. I do what I do, and they do what they do. We don't have a relationship. I'm the boss. They are the workers. I say what to do, and they do it.

I've witnessed this scene many times during my Lean journey. Weak, insecure "leaders" have so much pride and ego. They do it right in front of me and are proud of it. They don't know what they don't know. The previous example describes management of people. Telling people what to do is management, not leadership. A leader of people does things much differently.

As a leader, I would find a way to teach my team what I learned before we made any changes because I want their buy-in and their ideas. Plus, I would want us all to be on the same page. Then, we would have mini-kaizen events on the fly and improve the area together. I would do a lot of listening, learning, and asking questions if necessary, especially if I had an idea the team hadn't considered. Then, we would decide what to do together.

When necessary, I would explain the key things I had already learned in class. I would find a way to share the knowledge. Then, I would ask them questions and give them time to think about it and talk it over among themselves. I would want them to generate ideas because they will buy-in to their own ideas much faster and for much longer than they will buy-in to my ideas. Why? Because they want their ideas to work, and they have something to prove: they know how to make things better.

Leadership is about helping other people think at a higher level and helping them become responsible for improving themselves and their processes. Allowing them to provide solutions allows them to accept responsibility.

When you think of respect for the people, think of leadership principles. To demonstrate respect for the people, you must lead them. When you think of continuous improvement think of leadership principles supported by management principles. Always leadership first because influence is the foundation of action.

We *must* manage things, objects, and processes because they can't think and feel. Management is about competency. However, we *should* lead people because they do think and feel. People have the freedom to choose to follow or not to follow. Leadership is about character.

When we lead people, we respect them and treat them as volunteers because they are volunteers, no matter how much they are being paid while they are volunteering.

Associates don't have to do anything they don't want to do. They can quit and leave at any moment. However, most associates who report to managers, low impact leaders, do something much worse than quitting. They quit but stay. It's called disengagement. As a high impact Lean leader, your mission is to engage the disengaged.

You must lead people in such a way they choose to lead themselves well, they choose to lead others well, and they choose to manage their processes well. Lean is about people first and processes second.

Leadership is influence. With it, you will thrive. Without it, you will take a dive. When it comes to leadership, you must walk the talk. If you do, you will make deposits. If you don't, you will make withdrawals.

"When we are in the presence of good leadership, we usually are not even aware of it. Everything goes so well that leadership seems unnecessary; it creates the illusion that everything is seamless and smooth."
~ Jimmy Collins

19

PRIME THE PUMP

PREPARE THE TEAM FOR THE DREAM

*"Vision does not ignite growth, passion does. Passion
fuels vision, and vision is the focus of the power
of passion. Leaders who are passionate about
their call create vision." ~ Ken Hemphill*

High impact Lean leadership is about unleashing
people's potential, including your own.

Until you become more passionate about learning,
applying, and teaching the principles of leadership than
you are about learning, applying, and teaching the Lean
tools, you have not earned the title of high impact Lean
leader. High impact leadership is reserved for those who
leverage leadership to achieve exceptional results in their
area of passion and purpose.

In 2008, three years after beginning my journey as a
Lean leader, I discovered professional leadership
development content. I immediately knew leadership was
the missing Lean link. I knew it was the foundation for
respect for the people just as the Lean tools are the foundation
for *continuous improvement*. I was inspired to start reading
leadership books daily. Today, I still do. I will continue
reading daily for the rest of my life. There's a lot to learn.

I began my leadership journey listening to a condensed
one hour audio version of *The 7 Habits of Highly Effective
People* by Dr. Stephen R. Covey. Within the first few
minutes, I heard him say something that not only changed

the way I led Lean, especially kaizen events, but it also changed the way I lived my life because it changed the way I led myself.

Dr. Covey said, *"If you truly want to learn this material, start teaching it to others within 24-48 hours."* After listening to the entire audio, I knew I wanted to learn it. I've listened to it hundreds of times. The full-length version is actually 13 hours. But, all I needed was an overview to inspire me to become a lifetime student of leadership.

I didn't just listen to it and move on. I also followed his advice. He was the leadership expert. I was the Lean guy focused on the Lean tools. He knew what I didn't know. But, I knew I wanted to know what he knew. I immediately started teaching it to my family. I also realized each kaizen team every week was a captive audience.

Since I had never been taught what I was learning about leadership during my nearly 20 years in the blue-collar workforce, I thought most of those on the kaizen teams probably hadn't either. I also knew I got to decide what I would teach the teams I was leading.

Like most Lean leaders, I would always kick-off my events with a Lean overview as a refresher and to reveal the big picture for those new to Lean. I would mention continuous improvement and respect for the people briefly before diving deep into teaching the Lean tools we would be utilizing during the event. I've noticed most Lean leaders say them in that order too (CI & RFP).

I don't do it anymore. Today, I say respect for the people and then continuous improvement because respect for the people is the foundation for creating and sustaining a culture of continuous improvement.

During the first three years of leading Lean, I simply mentioned respect for the people briefly while discussing giving the people a voice, getting them involved in the process, etc. I didn't teach anything about leadership because I didn't know how to teach leadership. I just knew how to lead. Until I learned the language of leadership, I couldn't teach the principles of leadership.

I'm reminded of the words of Simon Sinek, *"We work to advance the vision of a leader who inspires us, and we work to undermine a dictator who means to control us."* In 2008, I began inspiring my kaizen teams by casting a vision for their future. I quit trying to control the people while using them as objects to implement Lean. I began allocating 20% of the time during any Lean event to leadership.

For example, on a 5-day event, I would open with four hours of leadership development and then open each of the remaining four days with an hour of leadership development. I discovered this inspired them. It made them feel valued. It made them feel like they mattered to me because they did. It made them feel good about the organization because the organization was paying me to be there. They truly felt respected. And, I connected.

Ultimately, it removed 99% of the resistance and prepared their minds for the week ahead. It's my hope that I can inspire you to adopt the 20/80 rule for your Lean events. 20% of the time dedicated to respect for the people, and 80% dedicated to continuous improvement.

You'll be amazed at the results. Go slow to go fast.

"Leaders who navigate do even more than control the direction in which they and their people travel. They see the whole trip in their minds before they leave the dock. They have a vision for their destination, they understand what it will take to get there, they know who they'll need on the team to be successful, and they recognize the obstacles long before they appear on the horizon." ~ John C. Maxwell

20

QUESTIONS TRANSFER RESPONSIBILITY

LEAD WITH QUESTIONS NOT DIRECTIONS

"When you initiate change, you take responsibility. Initiating change requires a proactive approach and only proactive people will do it. Initiating change requires you to say 'I will' instead of 'I wish.'"
~ Ria Story

Note: The content for this chapter is from my book, Blue-Collar Leadership & Supervision: Unleash Your Team's Potential.

There's a tremendous amount of power in a question. High impact Lean leaders leverage this power for many reasons by asking their teams A LOT of questions.

The primary reason managers of people ask questions is to position themselves to make better decisions. If they're asking a question, it is simply to gather only enough information to be used in their decision-making process.

The primary reason high impact leaders of people ask questions is to facilitate decision-making among their team members. They don't want to make all the decisions. They do want to grow and develop every member on their team and understand asking questions is one of the most effective ways to do that.

Here are seven reasons to ask effective, thought provoking questions.

7 Reasons to Ask Your Team Questions

1.   To show them respect. Asking questions demonstrates respect. It lets them know they matter and shows their opinions are valued and appreciated. It builds trust into the relationship. It allows the leader to model teamwork.

2.   To transfer influence to them. Asking questions allows them to influence the leader. It allows them to feel understood which creates more buy-in. When the team feels understood, they are more likely to support the path forward.

3.   To give them a voice. Asking questions allows the team to be involved in finding the solution. It allows them to have ownership in the process and the decision.

4.   To learn how they think. Asking questions is a valuable tool because it allows the leader to learn how each individual thinks. It allows the leader to learn which team members are ready and want to lead.

5.   To engage them in the process. Asking questions allows the leader to share the responsibility and engage the team. It gets team members involved who may otherwise keep their opinions to themselves. It empowers the team to act instead of being acted upon.

6.   To uncover hidden concerns. Asking questions allows team members to express concerns that may have otherwise remained unknown. It allows the leader to confirm the facts and minimize the rumors that spread so quickly along the front lines.

7.   To develop a better solution. Asking questions creates a synergistic environment which allows the leader to think with many minds instead of just one. It helps all team members to realize that none of them is as smart as all of them.

Questions allow you to steer the team as you grow and develop them. By asking the right questions at the right time in a group discussion, you can create teamwork. As you ask questions and the team develops solutions, always be sure to show gratitude to them as a team. Don't fall into the manager's trap of acknowledging only the person that comes up with the final solution. There are usually many thoughts that have been bounced around that created "group think," so acknowledge the group.

Questions also allow you to grow yourself as a leader. The better your questions are, the better the team's answers will be. Nguib Mahfouz expressed it this way, *"You can tell whether a man is clever by his answers. You can tell whether a man is wise by his questions."*

Great questions lead to great answers.

Don't miss the point. The power of the question is multiplied by your ability to listen and ask an impactful follow up question that allows the other person to dig a little deeper for a better answer or a totally different answer. It's the question after the question that often provides the best answer.

When team members ask a low impact leader a question, they get an answer. But when they ask a high impact leader a question, they get a question. It's a leader's job to grow their team. When we give them answers, we are not growing them. We are showing them. Be intentional. Answer more questions with questions. Questions make people think.

"It really is amazing what happens when you recognize the importance of the opportunities ahead of you, accept responsibility for your future, and take positive action." ~ Michael F. Sciortino, Sr.

21

AVOID ANSWERING QUESTIONS

DON'T MAKE DECISIONS;
FACILITATE DECISION MAKING

*"Some people assume we stumble
onto our success, but the path of discovery
is paved with interesting questions." ~ Bryan Cioffi*

I love leading kaizen teams. The main reason is because I love leading people through change and transformation. Another reason is because I get to ask a lot of questions. Often, I already know the answers to many of the questions I ask. Sometimes, I don't have a clue what the answer will be.

Why would I ask a question if I already know the answer? Because I want to allow team members to think for themselves and find their own answers. When they come up with the answer, I don't have to get them to buy-in to it. They already own it. However, if I give them the answer, it may be difficult to get them to buy-in. And, they may never buy-in. That's not the way to make things happen. I may think I know the answer when I don't really know the answer. Or, there may be more than one answer, and their answer may be better.

Allowing others to make decisions you could make demonstrates respect for the people.

Low impact Lean leaders have a habit of making decisions and giving directions. Leaders who do this don't know what they don't know about leadership. Most are not doing it with bad intentions. Many actually think they are helping by providing quick answers. Their intention is to help the team, not hinder the team. Some Lean leaders may have a pride and ego issue along with a desire to appear as if they know it all, but most don't.

Often, Lean leaders have been on many kaizen events with other teams. They have learned a lot and seen a lot. As a result, Lean leaders who don't know better attempt to accelerate things by giving directions and making decisions. They may be accelerating results short term, but they are slowing results long term.

Low impact Lean leaders are always thinking short term and seldom, if ever, think long term. Their focus is on the moment. Their focus is on achieving as much as possible during the kaizen event. Giving answers is going fast to go slow.

However, high impact Lean leaders are always thinking long term, not short term. Their focus is on the growth and development of others with the intent of creating a culture of kaizen. Asking questions is going slow to go fast. Giving others influence increases your influence.

If you want others to think for themselves, whether it's kaizen team members or your children, the first thing you must do is stop thinking for them. That means, if you want them to think for themselves, you must stop answering their questions. That isn't helping.

Asking others thought provoking questions will help them discover the answer if they are willing to think their way to it. Ask the question. Give them time to think.

When I'm training and developing Lean leaders, I always challenge them to learn to lead with questions. I say, *"Assume you have to lead the team only with questions."* Then, do it. Obviously, when you're teaching and communicating information you can't only ask questions.

But, once the event is underway, be intentional about leading with questions.

I remember leading a kaizen event in a production area. Two team members volunteered to look for ways to combine two separate pieces of equipment into one to allow for single-piece flow from one process step to the next without any wasted motion or transportation of material. It would be a big improvement.

Nearly an hour later, I was making my rounds and asking lots of questions. When I came upon these two, I asked, *"What have you come up with?"* I already had several ideas I hadn't shared. It wasn't about me figuring it out, it was about them figuring it out. They started telling me all the reasons it wouldn't work. They had a lot of reasons.

I didn't start thinking short term and give them a few tips by providing my ideas. I asked a question, *"Did you guys volunteer to figure out why it wouldn't work or how it could work?"* After a bit moaning and groaning, they admitted they agreed to figure out how to make it work. I asked, *"Are you still willing to do that?"* They both said yes. I gave them a thumbs up and began walking away.

Before I had walked 10 feet, one of them said, *"I know how we can do it."* and proceed to explain. I said, *"That will work. Is there another way?"* and turned to walk away. Instantly, the other guy said, *"I know another way."* and proceed to explain it. We all agreed either way would work. We now had at least two solutions. Success!

Their energy was focused on figuring out why it wouldn't work, but a few very simple questions redirected their thinking. I didn't offend them in any way. I didn't take the responsibility back. I lead them with questions.

> *"A humble ask can prompt an amazing feat."*
> *~ Liz Wiseman*

22

HIGH IMPACT DELEGATION

DELEGATE RESULTS NOT METHODS

"The more decisions a leader makes, the further he or she is away from leading a high performance team. Make too many command decisions and you'll doom yourself and your team to mediocrity." ~ Mark Miller

Note: The content for this chapter is from my book, 10 Values of High Impact Leaders, which has more information on delegation.

Delegation 101: Delegating *what to do*, makes you responsible. Delegating *what to accomplish*, allows others to become responsible. As Dr. Stephen R. Covey taught me so well, *"Never delegate methods, only results."*

High impact Lean leaders understand delegation is a tool for growing their team, strengthening relationships, transferring responsibility to others who are closer to the work being done, and allowing those closer to the problems to take ownership for solving the problems.

I've learned to be very effective at delegating. Not the old "do this and do that" kind of delegation most people think of when they hear the word delegation. That isn't leadership of people. That's management of people.

That's low level delegation and doesn't promote growth, responsibility, or ownership. High impact delegation empowers individuals and teams to thrive and grow. High impact delegation is about growth and development, not authority.

The 5 Levels of High Impact Delegation

1. Wait for Directions – No growth. No respect. No responsibility. A low impact leader simply tells the person or team what to do. The leader may not even be aware when the task finished. Either way, when they're finished, they wait for directions from the leader.

They keep waiting until they are told what to do next. This is absolutely the lowest level of delegation, and unfortunately, the most common. It's quick and efficient. It's also very effective, short term. Low impact leaders love it. It's also very ineffective and an absolute waste of time, long term. High impact leaders avoid it.

2. Ask, What's Next? – No growth. No respect. Only a very small amount of responsibility. The low impact leader instructs the person or team to ask what's next once they have completed the delegated task.

What small responsibility does the person or team have? When they are finished, they must find the leader and simply ask what's next. That's it. No growth and development at this level. The leader will see a slight increase in productivity because he/she is able to keep the person or team busy without as much waiting.

However, the leader still does all of the thinking and is responsible for determining what the person or team should and will do next. At least, the leader knows when they have completed their last assigned task. Then, another task can be assigned.

3. Recommend a Course of Action – Growth happens. Respect is mutual. Responsibility is transferred. Everything changes at this level. Thinking is now a shared responsibility. The leader values the person or team's experience, their opinions, and their decision making ability.

The responsibility for thinking, determining, and suggesting the next task is transferred to the person or team carrying out the task. They now must think before approaching the leader with a recommendation.

The leader is now in a support role growing and developing the person or team. As the leader learns to trust their thinking and decision making, he is able to move them to higher levels of delegation. If he doesn't yet trust them, he can continue asking questions to help shape and refine their thought process and understanding of the bigger picture.

4. Do It and Report Immediately – Additional, but limited, responsibility is transferred. The leader has more trust and confidence in the person or team and allows them to accept the responsibility of choosing, and then completing, the next task without support. Then, they notify the leader of what has been done before taking the next additional action.

5. Own It and Report Routinely – Full responsibility has been transferred. At this level, the person or team reports to the leader at predetermined intervals such as: the end of a project, a specific number of days, weeks, months, or when the person or team feels it is necessary. The leader trusts the person or team completely and is confident in their ability to make the right decisions.

As Ken Allen commented, *"Rarely is delegation failure the subordinate's fault. Maybe you picked the wrong person for the job, didn't train, develop, or motivate sufficiently."* I don't agree with the term subordinate, but I do agree with the rest of Ken's comment. Effective delegation is the leader's responsibility.

> *"In a culture of discipline, people do not have jobs; they have responsibilities." ~ Jim Collins*

23

WHERE'S THE PROBLEM?

GO SEE, DEMONSTRATE RESPECT, AND ASK QUESTIONS

"Lean managers pose questions to their problem owners about the nature of the problem and the best available counter-measures. Doing this automatically transfers responsibility for the problem...closer to the problem." ~ *Jim Womack*

Questions are a high impact Lean leader's best friend. That's why there are five chapters dedicated to revealing why you should use questions and how you can use questions to leverage your influence and increase buy-in.

"Where's the problem?" is one of my favorite questions to ask kaizen team members. Most often, they don't know the answer. Most often, the problem is in the mirror. They are usually the problem. The way they are thinking or the fact that they are not thinking is usually the problem. They just don't know it.

After a day or two together, the entire team catches on and starts having a little fun calling each other out by asking each other, *"Where's the problem?"* and receiving a quick answer from their teammate, *"In the mirror."*

Having fun is one of the objectives I discuss when I kick-off an event. And, we always achieve that objective. Having fun is another way to connect with the team members, and it helps them connect with each other.

I also ask, *"Where's the problem?"* when the team is

attempting to search for the root cause while sitting in an office or looking at a computer. I ask the question because I want them to go to where the problem is happening to figure out the root cause of the problem with those closest to the problem.

The question usually leads them out the office door to find the answer. If you want to find out what's really happening and what's causing it to happen, you must go to the Gemba, the actual place where the work happens or the problem is occurring.

High impact Lean leaders know the value of going to see. I don't depend on reports or data in a database because I already know that information is most likely inaccurate. I don't trust it. I don't care how many people in the room say it is accurate, or it's been verified.

Based on my experience, I always learn something when I go see for myself and ask questions while I'm there. The last thing I want to do is be responsible for decisions based on bad information from someone who isn't responsible. I'm always responsible. I always want to go see. I want to know. I don't want to think I know.

Whenever I ask questions during a kaizen event, I often follow up after I get the answer with another question, *"Do you really know, or do you think you know?"* If they answer is, *"Yes, I know."* I follow up with another question, *"How do you know?"* It doesn't take long after asking that question to determine if they really know or if they think they know.

Many of the problems in organizations have the same root cause: people making decisions based on bad information they believe is true because it was in the system or because they were told something by someone who didn't know but thought they knew.

Trust me. Take the time it takes, so it takes less time.

Go to the source. Demonstrate respect. Ask questions.

One of the first things I teach kaizen team members is the Lean meaning of *"Why?"* I explain the meaning before they start asking the questions at the Gemba because I want the team to teach those at the Gemba the Lean meaning of *"Why?"* too. What I'm really doing and asking them to do is to declare their intent before asking *"Why?"* Declaring intent helps us demonstrate respect.

I teach the *why* lesson by letting the team teach themselves. How? By asking questions. I ask, *"When a boss walks up and asks why you are doing something, what does it usually mean?"* Often, someone will say, *"It means they think I'm doing it wrong."* Or, someone will say, *"It means they think I shouldn't be doing it."* They are right because in a traditional environment, that is what it means most often.

Then, I ask, *"If a young child walks up and asks why you are doing something, what does it usually mean?"* Right away, someone will answer, *"It means they want to know why you are doing it. They want to learn."* I say, *"Exactly!"*

Next I ask, *"If I ask you why you're doing something, or if I ask someone working in the plant why they are doing something, why am I asking?"* I always get the perfect answer, *"Because you want to learn."*

After the priming the pump, they are ready and open to being asked *why*. When I hear them teaching others on the plant floor, I know they learned the lesson and are demonstrating respect. They know my intent because I let them think it through. They know my intention is to learn, not to blame. Questions are powerful.

"Solving complex problems requires an inquiring mind and the willingness to experiment one's way to a fresh solution." ~ Daniel Pink

24

THE POWER OF HOW

THE BEST LEADERS
ASK THE BEST QUESTIONS

*"Certainty is one of the weakest positions in life.
Curiosity is one of the most powerful.
Certainty prohibits learning; curiosity fuels change."
~ Dr. Henry Cloud*

The three letters that will allow you to learn the most are W-H-Y. The three letters that will inspire others to think the most are H-O-W.

High impact Lean leaders intentionally weave these small but powerful words into many of their questions.

Asking *"Why?"* produces knowledge.

Asking *"How?"* produces solutions.

Note: The following is an excerpt from the book, Change Happens: Leading Yourself and Others through Change, that I co-authored with my wife Ria. Teach this to your kaizen teams.

When it comes to embracing change, there's a magic word you can proactively use to begin separating yourself from the crowd in a way that allows you to get noticed by the high impact leaders and promoted for the right reasons. The magic word is "HOW?" Before I tell you how to use the magic word, I want to share a few thoughts with you.

Fear of change will create self-doubt if you choose to be reactive instead of proactive. When you choose to be reactive, you begin to look for the negative impact the change will have on you, whether it's at work or at home. Reactive people quickly become the victim of change.

As you begin to think of all the different ways change is going to negatively impact you, your imagination begins to run wild in the wrong direction. When this happens, you are no longer in control. You're out of control and along for the ride.

However, when you embrace change, you are also embracing responsibility. When you embrace responsibility, you are being proactive. This is where the magic word truly becomes magical. When change happens, proactive people do not immediately begin to ask, *"What's going to happen?"* They leverage the magic word: HOW?

Listen to the voices of those proactively embracing change:

- How would a proactive person respond?
- How will I be viewed if I respond positively?
- How can I help others embrace the change?
- How will this benefit me?
- How can I leverage this change to my benefit?
- How will this benefit our team?
- How will this benefit the organization?
- How will this make us more competitive?
- How can I help make it happen?

I captured this quote while reading one of Ria's books. She said, *"If we embrace the chance of living life to the fullest, then we must be willing to accept responsibility for doing it."* If we're going to embrace change and become responsible for leading ourselves and others through change effectively, we must be willing to use the magic word: HOW?

When you ask, *"How can I?"* or *"How can we?"* instead of *"Can I?"* or *"Can we?"* you have started to truly transform the way you and others think.

"Can I?" or *"Can we?"* indicates self-doubt.

You don't know if you or the team can. But, when you ask *"How can I?"* or *"How can we?"* you have already decided you will and you can. Therefore, your imagination can run wild in the right direction. *"How can I?"* or *"How can we?"* indicates there is a way. You just need to discover it.

Asking how triggers the proactive muscles in your mind, and you get busy trying to find a way. You'll discover there's often more than one way.

Reactive people are very stuck. Stuck playing the role of victim. Proactive people are very creative. Once you choose to embrace change, you are positioned to begin leveraging change for your benefit.

Ask yourself.

How can I embrace change? How can I begin to recognize the importance of change? How can I accept responsibility for change? How can I leverage change for my benefit?

And most importantly, how can I take positive action when change happens?

Once I learned to put *how* in front of *can*, I engaged all of those participating on the kaizen teams at an entirely new level. I didn't just ask *how?* I declared intent and primed the pump by teaching them the *how* principle on opening day during the leadership development training.

"When you want to persuade, you'll always get further by asking a question than by making a statement."
~ Dorothy Leeds

25

LEAD THE TEAM

UNLEASH THE TEAM'S POTENTIAL

"All leaders know there's a huge gap between what the team has to do and what the team is capable of doing. High impact leaders close the gap. Low impact leaders widen the gap."
~ Mack Story

If you want those on your kaizen teams to do more and be better, during and after the event, then you must do more and get better before the event.

There's one thing I know about you even if I've never met you. You are getting the exact results you're supposed to be getting. If you were supposed to be getting different results, you would be getting different results. Where's the problem? Trust me. It's in the mirror.

I always say, *"If the team isn't performing, it's because the leader isn't serving."* What does this mean exactly? Who should you be serving? High impact leaders believe they are supposed to serve the team. Low impact leaders believe the team is supposed to serve them.

Some people don't like the word serve, especially those in the blue-collar workforce. They think serving means you're soft. Serve is simply a synonym for help. I could just as easily have said, *"If the team isn't performing, it's because the leader isn't helping."* Leadership is about helping others accomplish the mission. Helping is serving.

Since leadership is influence and everyone has

influence, everyone is a leader. People are simply leading (influencing) at different levels. As a high impact Lean leader, your personal mission should be to help increase the influence (leadership) of everyone on a kaizen team at the minimum and everyone in the organization at the maximum. Yes, everyone.

You can't lead those beyond your leadership level. You can't develop leaders beyond your own level. People naturally follow leaders who are on their level or above, but they don't generally follow people who are on a lower level unless there's a specific reason to follow them.

What determines your leadership level? Primarily your character. Secondarily your competency. If you're leading a kaizen event, who you are matters first. What you know about Lean matters second. If you're selling me a car, who you are matters first. What you know about the product and the purchasing process, matters second.

Remember the 87/13 principle. Remember the two components of trust: character and competency. If the people don't like you and don't connect with you for whatever reason, it doesn't really matter how much you know. You won't be able to get meaningful results repeatedly. You'll be considered a low performer.

If you want to lead at a higher level, you must intentionally move beyond your position or title. You must focus on building relationships. The stronger and more developed your character is, the stronger and more meaningful your relationships will be.

Once you have strong, meaningful relationships, you can only leverage them if you have a competency that provides value to others. As a Lean leader, this means you must know about the Lean tools and how to apply them.

If you can quickly build strong trusting relationships with kaizen team members, they will want to follow you.

You are positioned for success. However, you must also be able to effectively understand, teach, and apply the principles related to the Lean tools. If you can do this well, you will get good results consistently.

Do you want good results or exceptional results? If you want exceptional results, you must get the team to go to an entirely different level with you. This book is meant to help you get them to the next level. But, you can't raise the bar for others if you can't reach it yourself.

The key is influencing them to do more than required. How do you that? Learn to apply what's in this book. When the team does what is required, they will produce good results. Any Lean leader should be able to deliver good results. When teams consistently and repeatedly do much more than is required, they are producing exceptional results. Only high impact Lean leaders can help their team deliver exceptional results.

In order to influence your team to deliver exceptional results, you must first be an exceptional Lean leader. You must have exceptional character. You must have exceptional knowledge of the Lean tools. But, that's not enough. You must also do more than is required. There's one more thing you must add to the mix.

You must do something for the team that isn't required of you. You must invest in them because they are people you care about, not because they are kaizen team members. When you invest in them as I've been teaching you to do in this book, they will feel it. When they feel it, you will be leading an exceptional team.

> *"Coming together is a beginning.*
> *Keeping together is progress.*
> *Working together is success."*
> *~ Henry Ford*

26

LEVERAGE THE TEAM

FOCUS ON STRENGTHS; DEVELOP WEAKNESSES

"Instead of focusing on weaknesses, give your attention to people's strengths. Focus on sharpening skills that already exist. Compliment positive qualities. Bring out the gifts inherent in them. Weaknesses can wait unless they are character flaws. Only after you have developed a strong rapport with the person and they have begun to grow and gain confidence should you address areas of weakness... and then those should be handled gently and one at a time."
~ *John C. Maxwell*

High impact Lean leaders have a gift for turning a group of people into a team in a short period of time.

At the start of a kaizen event, calling the group of people a team is a poor use of the word team. They are simply a group of people assembled in a room about to be given a task to accomplish together. Most often, some want to be there, and some don't want to be there. Odds are, this specific group of people has never worked together on a project before.

Knowing about continuous improvement is a must if you're going to lead a kaizen event. However, knowing about continuous improvement (your competency) will not be the key to turning a group of people into a team of people. Turning a group of people into a team of people is about having respect for the people. Your ability to quickly build a strong, functional team will be determined primarily by your character and secondarily by your competency. Your character is key in this area.

I've seen some very talented Lean leaders and others who have an extensive in-depth knowledge of Lean attempt to lead kaizen events. Most often, they struggle from the moment the event kicks off until the end. They know a lot about Lean but very little about leading people effectively. Why? Because their focus has been on learning Lean, not on learning leadership.

When it comes to growing, developing, and creating a new team, high impact Lean leaders know to focus on the team members' strengths in their area of competency and to focus on their weaknesses in the area of character.

Each team member's competency strengths (what they know and can do), if leveraged, will launch the team forward. Each team member's character weaknesses (who they are) will hold the team back. This includes you.

High impact Lean leaders know there are always character issues. We all have them. A few of us are constantly working to improving ourselves, but many of us aren't. Focusing on character weaknesses is why high impact Lean leaders blend leadership development and personal growth components into all of their continuous improvement initiatives.

This is why I utilize the 20/80 rule I taught you in chapter 19. I didn't start using it by accident. I started using it by design. Until then, I only focused on leveraging the team's strengths. But, I hadn't been focused on developing their weaknesses. I'm sure you already know the root cause of most major problems that arise during kaizen events, whether with team members or people not on the team, is rooted in character issues.

The majority of Lean leaders focus only on the continuous improvement (competency) component of Lean. As a result, they provide no leadership in the area that will hold them and the team back the most, character development.

The reason Lean leaders do not address character development during kaizen events is because most, if not all, of them are not addressing it in their own life. In other words, because they are not leading themselves well, they can't lead others well. Character development is always the missing link personally and professionally.

In the area of competency, ask questions and generate discussions to find out what people like or don't like to do. Don't assume they like to do what they are paid to do. I always have everyone introduce and speak about themselves before I talk about anything. I ask what their job is, how long they have been with the organization, what their previous job was, what their hobbies are, what they do for fun, how much Lean and event experience they have, and I ask them to tell me about their family.

The answers to these questions and the associated discussions allow me to connect and learn about their strengths. Then, I'm positioned to leverage the team.

"Humility means knowing and using your strength for the benefit of others, on behalf of a higher purpose. The humble leader is not weak, but strong...is not pre-occupied with self, but with how best to use his or her strengths for the good of others. A humble leader does not think less of himself, but chooses to consider the needs of others in fulfilling a worthy cause. We love to be in the presence of a humble leader because they bring out the very best in us. Their focus is on our purpose, our contribution, and our ability to accomplish all we set out to accomplish." ~ Alan Ross

27

EXPAND THE TEAM

HARNESS THE INFLUENCE OF THE TEAM TO GAIN SUPPORT FOR THE TEAM

"The most valuable player is the one that makes the most players valuable." ~ Peyton Manning

There's a lot of influence on every kaizen team. As a high impact Lean leader, it's your responsibility to leverage the team's influence. By leveraging the cumulative influence of the team, you're able to generate additional support and buy-in for the team's mission far beyond your normal circle of influence.

Making leadership development and personal growth a component of your Lean initiative will pay huge dividends as your efforts to invest in the development of people are compounded over time. When you invest in people because they are people, the connection will create many mutually beneficial, long term relationships.

People throughout the organization with a positive mindset will be attracted to who you are and your mission. They will want to help you because you have helped them not only professionally, but also personally. You will develop far reaching relationships through all departments and at all levels.

Adding the leadership development component to your Lean initiative and all of the kaizen events you lead or facilitate while training others to lead is crucial relative expanding each team beyond the team. First, choose to invest time teaching the team principles that will help them have a better life not only at work, but also at home (instead of jumping right in to Lean training and/or going to the Gemba to get busy). The team will pay you back through support during and after the event. They will gladly loan you their influence when you need it.

I can also warn you that low impact leaders (managers of people) throughout the organization will not support adding the leadership development component to the Lean initiative in general or as a 20% component of kaizen events. Low impact leaders are focused on the process, not the people.

Low impact leaders, whether leading Lean or in other leadership roles, don't want to go slow to go fast. Their preferred method is going fast to go slow. I've seen them rolling their eyes and heard them making negative remarks about the leadership training on Monday mornings many times during the many events I've led.

I ignore them publically and attempt to work with them privately, if they're open to it. Some come around simply from going through the leadership training during the event. Some never come around. Either way, I'm responsible for getting buy-in from the team for a bigger mission: creating a culture of kaizen. The low impact leaders are only worried about the short term mission.

You must always focus on the big picture because you will need all the help you can get along your Lean journey. When you have a large pool of people voluntarily following you, you indirectly influence the people they influence as well.

For example, I may not be able to influence the maintenance manager into dedicating a team member to my kaizen event for a week. He doesn't report to me, and doesn't have to do what I say. He may simply say, *"I'm glad to help when you need it. Just give us a call. But, I can't dedicate a person to the team all week, we've got too much going on."*

If that's his reply, there may not be much I can do. He has provided himself and his team member a way out because he is offering support, and everyone knows he and his team are busy. Everyone is always busy.

Going to his boss and forcing him to dedicate someone to the team won't be a deposit. It will be a withdrawal. However, if I have a strong relationship with someone who has a strong relationship with the maintenance manager or even a maintenance team member, I can often use their influence to gain buy-in.

How? I get them to sell the leader on supporting the team. The leader may not do it for me, but he may do it for someone who has more influence with him. That's one way to allow others to help get people on the team.

But, what about making things happen during the event? Your kaizen team will be full of people with wide reaching influence. Part of getting to know them is getting to know who they know. Allow them to lead the way in asking for support from those who can help or who work in a department with resources the team needs.

Once you've invested in growing the team and they know your heart and know your mission is to help the people, they will answer and offer help when you ask, *"Who knows somebody who can help us make it happen?"*

"Sometimes the more you know, the less you learn...Too often we play solo when we should be gathering the support of a broader team. Too often we drown out new voices with cynicism, blunt criticism, and explanations for why their ideas won't fly."
~ Liz Wiseman

28

LEVERAGE THE LEADERS

MAXIMIZE THE INFLUENCE OF THE LEADERS WHO SUPPORT YOU

"If you could get all the people in an organization rowing in the same direction, you could dominate any industry, in any market, against any competition, at any time." ~ Patrick Lencioni

Gaining the support of the formal leaders in your organization will accelerate the organization's Lean journey. As you focus more on the respect for the people foundational layer of Lean, you will also position yourself as a resource for developing the formal leaders and their teams within the organization.

Most often, organizations interested in leadership development don't get their leadership support from a Lean leader. They seek out a leadership expert. They see leadership and Lean as two different professions because they usually are. However, they shouldn't be.

A leadership expert doesn't need to be a Lean expert. However, in order to be a high impact Lean leader, you must be both: a Lean expert and a leadership expert.

In organizations where leadership development is not a part of who they are and what they do, it will be easier to position yourself as the leadership development expert too. Most often, no one has taken responsibility for leadership development because few, if any, leaders have been exposed to formal leadership development or have an interest in it. Primarily because they don't know what they don't know. You can change that.

I've discussed repeatedly the value of adding a leadership development component to your kaizen events. However, you should also position yourself as the leadership development resource throughout the organization. However, you can't do this if you haven't been reading, studying, and applying leadership principles in your own life first.

If you haven't been investing time and resources in your own development, start there. Then, as you begin to learn and master principles start teaching them to others directly and indirectly. Kaizen events are the perfect place to train yourself and others. That's exactly what I did. I was teaching my teams what I was learning while I was learning it. I told them, *"We're going to learn together."*

As you get comfortable, you may have leaders who are on your teams ask you to train them and/or their team members on something you taught during an event. Or, they may ask you to conduct more in-depth training. The key is to use your influence to become the leadership resource beyond the kaizen events.

By developing leadership development not only for the formal leaders at all levels, but also for their teams you will be building strong relationships with the leaders who have a tremendous amount of influence they can use to speed you up or slow you down. It depends on how they feel about you.

If you've been helping them develop the character of the people who report to them, you are helping eliminate or reduce people problems. Do this and you will have a lot of new followers. You will be leading the leaders who will be happy to choose to follow you.

Create and promote leadership development

programs, so others will know what you offer. I offer certifications with an independent license to teach my content complete with a pre-developed training kit for any of my books. You can learn more about this at www.BlueCollarLeaders.com/certifications if you have an interest and need help jump starting your program.

My intent is to give Lean leaders a head start by letting them stand on my shoulders as I have stood on the shoulders of others. We are on this journey together.

Imagine you are the resource for leadership development throughout the organization and are applying my 20/80 rule on all of your kaizen events. You will have so much support from the high impact leaders within the organization that you will struggle to keep up with demand for your time relative to Lean and leadership. Trust me. I have lived through it repeatedly.

However, most Lean leaders struggle to get buy-in and support for what they are trying to accomplish. Many formal leaders within organizations do what they have to do and not a bit more when it comes to supporting Lean. If you take responsibility for executing what I've been teaching you throughout this book, you will begin to transform the culture of the organization and the character of the leaders within the organization.

Once you do, you will have built a team of formal leaders who are helping you lead Lean. The more you focus on leading the leaders, the more the leaders will focus on leading themselves and others. You don't need a position or title to lead the leaders. You simply need a desire and a passion to develop yourself and others.

"It is a big step in your development when you come to realize that other people can help you do a better job than you could do alone." ~ Andrew Carnegie

29

THE KEY TO SUCCESS

HIGH IMPACT LEADERS MUST KNOW THE WAY, SHOW THE WAY, AND GO THE WAY

"Try not to become men of success.
Rather, become men of value." ~ Albert Einstein

Choosing to become the leader of the leaders is a big responsibility. However, the same character traits that will cause kaizen team members to choose to follow you will be the same character traits that will cause other leaders to choose to follow you. Who you are matters.

You'll discover high impact leaders are real, authentic, trustworthy people with high integrity. They will also follow lower level leaders to intentionally develop them and to help give them the confidence to lead. They may or may not have a title or a high level position. If they do, they tend to see their position and title as a platform for growing and developing people.

Becoming a confident high impact leader of leaders will require you to become comfortable being uncomfortable. High impact Lean leadership will cause you discomfort at times. All of your growth will happen outside of your comfort zone. If you're not uncomfortable, you're not growing, you're coasting. As Denis G. McLaughlin remarked, *"Leadership isn't about your comfort. It's about your commitment."*

From one high impact Lean leader to another, I'm

asking you to make a commitment to first lead yourself at a higher level, and then, to lead others to a higher level.

When people start learning what high impact leadership looks and feels like, they typically don't look in the mirror to judge themselves. Instead, they most often look out the window and judge the leaders they report to or leaders who work in their organization. They especially look out the window and judge the leader that's teaching them leadership. They shouldn't, but they do.

One of your leadership objectives should be to get people to stop looking out the window and to start looking in the mirror. In order to do that, you must change what they see when they look out the window at you and other leaders. They will look out the window. It's what people do. If they see you teaching one thing but living something else, your credibility will be lost. You can't be a high impact leader without rock solid credibility. Credibility is a must for trust.

Teaching leadership is different than teaching Lean. Lean is a methodology for improving processes. Leadership is a way of being. Therefore, when you teach leadership, your credibility will be based on the degree to which you live what you are teaching. How are you being?

Your leadership of yourself is vital to your own success and the success of the leaders in your organization. If you're anything like I was, you may need to do more than make a few changes. You may have to transform yourself at the core as I did. If you discover or already feel that's the case, you will definitely want to check out my book, *10 Foundational Elements of Intentional Transformation: How to Become Your Best Self*, because you will need some help. And, I'll be glad to help you.

You don't have to be perfect, but you must be serious about attempting to live what you are asking others to live. You must be serious about trying to be as you are asking others to be. Just as you teach people to see waste through "Lean glasses," you will be teaching people to see character through "leadership glasses."

Lean development helps people see process flaws. Leadership development helps people see character flaws.

As Simon Sinek stated so well, *"Short or long term, the clearer we can see what we are setting out to achieve, the more likely we are to achieve it."* You pick an area to pilot when you're beginning a Lean transformation, so the people will have a model of what to expect. As a high impact leader, you must model high level character, so others will know what high impact leadership looks and feels like.

A leader's character determines the behavior they will model for others to follow, the behavior they will accept, the type of people they will attract to their team, and the type of individuals who will remain on their team. A leader's character will also determine if they will or won't create a formal leadership development program to align everyone around a common language and core set of guiding principles and beliefs.

Low impact leaders dodge responsibility by simply expecting their team to know how to behave. That would be great if every person had the same core beliefs and life experiences to shape them into what the leader expects them to be. However, everyone is different and has different experiences, values, and expectations.

High impact leaders create the environment that will support the culture they intentionally create through modeling, training, and development. They accept the responsibility of high impact leadership. Will you?

"True leadership only exists if people follow when they have the freedom not to." ~ *Jim Collins*

87

30

SUSTAIN THE GAIN

WHEN YOU INVEST IN THE PEOPLE, THEY WILL INVEST IN THE PROCESS

*"Not investing in your people to save money
is like cutting a leg off to save weight.
Initially, it achieves your short term goal,
but the long term effects are disastrous."
~ Sid Joynson*

The biggest challenge of Lean has always been sustaining the gain. Until organizational leaders and Lean leaders make people development the foundational layer of their culture, sustaining the gain will continue to be an unachieveable goal.

My hope as I begin to write this last chapter is that you choose to become more than a Lean champion in your organization. I hope my words have inspired you to look in the mirror and do some reflecting on who you are and how you lead Lean. I hope you become a high impact Lean champion with a heavier focus on respect for the people in an effort to inspire and sustain a culture of kaizen. The people need you to step up to the next level.

If you were not a student of leadership development and personal growth before reading this book, I hope you choose to become one. The blue-collar industries are filled with amazing people who have unlimited potential. Without a high impact leader to lead the way, most will never know who they could have become and what they could have achieved. They need you to lead them.

Although I have the privilege of teaching and speaking about leadership to white-collar and blue-collar people at all levels from top to bottom, my greatest passion is developing those on the front lines of the blue-collar workforce. I hope you've felt that in my words. I hope you share the same passion. They need our help.

Too often, when I speak to leaders about developing their people, the first question they ask is, *"What's the ROI (return on investment)? Or, how do we measure the payback?"* As soon as I hear those words, I know I won't likely be developing their people because the leader sees it as business decision not a leadership decision. For them, it's about respect for the profits, not respect for the people.

On the other hand, high impact leaders never mention ROI. They know as I do, it doesn't matter. They do it because of their character, not because of the ROI. If there is truly respect for the people, you don't invest in the development of the people for the ROI. You do it because they matter.

As Captain L. David Marquet stated so accurately, *"Greatness is achieved by using resources to help people; not using people as a resource."* You know the words of a high impact leader when you hear them, because you can feel them.

Many companies throw away more money in scrap product in a day than they invest in their people through leadership development in a year. They see the people only as the resource for producing profits. They don't see profits as a resource for developing people who can help increase profits. As a result, they get the results they are aligned to get.

As a high impact Lean leader, to accomplish your mission in a way that not only sustains the gain, but also creates an engaged workforce that is thriving in a culture of kaizen, you must increase your influence and leverage the corporate resources (time and money) in order to intentionally develop the people.

When high impact leaders invest in the people on the front lines, the people become equipped and inspired to help improve the bottom line. When people are valued, they become more valuable. When people are cared for, they care for those who care for them.

I'm reminded of the words of Terry A. Smith, *"Every wise leader, whether a manager, a military officer, or a mother — should consider how to lead those who follow him or her as if inspiration were the only leadership leverage. Good leaders inspire people. They breathe life into individuals and groups. They animate organizations. They breed the contagion of enthusiasm. They excite people to dream the dreams, take the risks, and make the sacrifices that are necessary to create better futures."*

Respect for the people begins with you.

The people don't need to hear it.

The people need to feel it.

"If Lean is done wrong, and there is entirely a tools focus, and we're beating up the people, and we need results, and it's all about the numbers, it's not going to sustain itself, which many companies have proved."
~ Jerry Solomon

I welcome hearing how this book has influenced the way you think, the way you lead, or the results you have achieved because of what you've learned in it. Please feel free to share your thoughts with me by email at:

Mack@MackStory.com

To order my books and other resources, please visit:
TopStoryLeadership.com or Amazon.

ABOUT THE AUTHOR

Mack's story is an amazing journey of personal and professional growth. He married Ria in 2001. He has one son, Eric, born in 1991.

After graduating high school in 1987, Mack joined the United States Marine Corps Reserve as an 0311 infantryman. Soon after, he began his 20 plus year manufacturing career. Graduating with highest honors, he earned an Executive Bachelor of Business Administration degree from Faulkner University.

Mack began his career in manufacturing in 1988 on the front lines of a large production machine shop. He eventually grew himself into upper management and found his niche in lean manufacturing and along with it, developed his passion for leadership. In 2008, he launched his own Lean Manufacturing and Leadership Development firm.

From 2005-2012, Mack led leaders and their cross-functional teams through more than 11,000 hours of process improvement, organizational change, and cultural transformation. Ria joined Mack in 2013.

In 2013, they worked with John C. Maxwell as part of an international training event focused on the Cultural Transformation in Guatemala where over 20,000 leaders were trained. They also shared the stage with internationally recognized motivational speaker Les Brown in 2014.

Mack and Ria have published nearly 20 books on personal growth and leadership development and publish more each year. In 2017, they reached 50,000 international followers on LinkedIn where they provide daily motivational, inspirational, and leadership content to people all over the world.

Some of their clients: ATD (Association for Talent Development), Auburn University, Brose, Chick-fil-A, EXIT Realty, Kimberly Clark, Koch Industries, Southern Company.

Mack is an inspiration for people everywhere as an example of achievement, growth, and personal development. His passion motivates and inspires people all over the world!

TOP STORY LEADERSHIP

- ✓ Keynote Speaking
- ✓ Leadership Development
- ✓ Blue-Collar Leadership Development
- ✓ On-site Half-day/Full-day Workshops/Seminars
- ✓ Corporate Retreats
- ✓ Limited one-on-one coaching/mentoring
- ✓ On-site Lean Leadership Certification
- ✓ Lean Leader Leadership Development
- ✓ Become licensed to teach our content

For more information please visit:

www.TopStoryLeadership.com

www.BlueCollarLeaders.com

www.LinkedIn.com/in/MackStory

www.LinkedIn.com/in/RiaStory

Excerpt from
Defining Influence

In *Defining Influence*, I outline the foundational leadership principles and lessons we must learn in order to develop our character in a way that allows us to increase our influence with others. I also share many of my personal stories revealing how I got it wrong many times in the past and how I grew from front-line factory worker to become a Leadership Expert.

INTRODUCTION

"Leadership is influence. Nothing more. Nothing less. Everything rises and falls on leadership."
~ John C. Maxwell

Everyone is born a leader.

I haven't always believed everyone is a leader. You may or may not at this point. That's okay. There is a lot to learn about leadership.

At this very moment, you may already be thinking to yourself, "I'm not a leader." My goal is to help you understand why everyone is a leader and to help you develop a deeper understanding of the principles of leadership and influence.

Developing a deep understanding of leadership, has changed my life for the better. It has also changed the lives of my family members, friends, associates, and clients. I want to help you improve not only your life, but also the lives of those around you.

Until I became a student of leadership which eventually led me to become a John Maxwell Team Certified Leadership Coach, Trainer, and Speaker, and author, I did not understand leadership or realize everyone can benefit from learning the related principles.

In the past, I thought leadership was a term associated with being the boss and having formal authority over others.

Those people are definitely leaders. But, I had been missing something. All of the other seven billion people on the planet are leaders too.

Why do I say everyone is born a leader? I agree with John Maxwell, "Leadership is Influence. Nothing more. Nothing less." Everyone has influence. It's a fact. Therefore, everyone is a leader.

No matter your age, gender, religion, race, nationality, location, or position, everyone has influence. Whether you want to be a leader or not, you are. After reading this book, I hope you do not question whether or not you are a leader. However, I do hope you question what type of leader you are and what level leader you are.

Everyone does not have authority, but everyone does have influence. There are plenty of examples in the world of people without authority leading people through influence alone. Actually, every one of us is an example. We have already done it. We know it is true. This principle is self-evident which means it contains its own evidence and does not need to be demonstrated or explained; it is obvious to everyone.

The question to ask is not, "Are you a leader?" The question is, "What type of leader are you?" The answer: whatever kind you choose to be. Choosing not to be a leader is not an option. As long as you live, you will have influence. You are a leader.

You had influence before you were born and may have influence after your death. How? Thomas Edison still influences the world every time a light is turned on, you may do things in your life to influence others long after you're gone. Or, you may pass away with few people noticing. It depends on the choices you make.

Even when you're alone, you have influence. The most important person you will ever influence is yourself. The degree to which you influence yourself determines the level of influence you ultimately have with others. Typically, when we are talking about leading ourselves, the word most commonly used to describe self-leadership is discipline which can be defined as giving yourself a command and following through with it. We must practice discipline daily to increase our influence with others. It is not something we do only when we feel like it.

"We must all suffer one of two things: the pain of discipline or the pain of regret or disappointment."
~ Jim Rohn

As I define leadership as influence, keep in mind the word leadership and influence can be interchanged anytime and anyplace. They are one and the same. Throughout this book, I'll help you remember by placing one of the words in parentheses next to the other occasionally as a reminder. They are synonyms. When you read one, think of the other.

Everything rises and falls on influence (leadership). When you share what you're learning, clearly define leadership as influence for others. They need to understand the context of what you are teaching and understand they *are* leaders (people with influence) too. If you truly want to learn and apply leadership principles, you must start teaching this material to others within 24-48 hours of learning it yourself.

You will learn the foundational principles of leadership (influence) which will help you understand the importance of the following five questions. You will be able to take effective action by growing yourself and possibly others to a higher level of leadership (influence). Everything you ever achieve, internally and externally, will be a direct result of your influence.

1. ***Why* do we influence?** – Our character determines *why* we influence. Who we are on the inside is what matters. Do we manipulate or motivate? It's all about intent.

2. ***How* do we influence?** – Our character, combined with our competency, determines *how* we influence. Who we are and what we know combine to create our unique style of influence which determines our methods of influence.

3. **Where** do we influence? – Our passion and purpose determine *where* we have the greatest influence. What motivates and inspires us gives us the energy and authenticity to motivate and inspire others.

4. **Who** do we influence? – We influence those *who* buy-in to us. Only those valuing and seeking what we value and seek will volunteer to follow us. They give us or deny us permission to influence them based on how well we have developed our character and competency.

5. **When** do we influence? – We influence others *when* they want our influence. We choose when others influence us. Everyone else has the same choice. They decide when to accept or reject our influence. We only influence others when they want to change.

The first three questions are about the choices we make as we lead (influence) ourselves and others. The last two questions deal more with the choices others will make as they decide first, *if* they will follow us, and second, *when* they will follow us. They will base their choices on *who we are* and *what we know*.

Asking these questions is important. Knowing the answers is more important. But, taking action based on the answers is most important. Cumulatively, the answers to these questions determine our leadership style and our level of influence (leadership).

On a scale of 1-10, your influence can be very low level (1) to very high level (10). But make no mistake, you *are* a leader. You *are* always on the scale. The higher on the scale you are the more effective you are. You will be at different levels with different people at different times depending on many different variables.

Someone thinking they are not a leader or someone that doesn't want to be a leader, is still a leader. They will simply remain a low level leader with low level influence getting low level results. They will likely spend much time frustrated with many areas of their life. Although they could influence a change, they choose instead to be primarily influenced by others.

What separates higher level leaders from lower level leaders? There are many things, but two primary differences are:

1) Higher level leaders accept more responsibility in all areas of their lives while lower level leaders tend to blame others and transfer responsibility more often.

2) Higher level leaders have more positive influence while lower level leaders tend to have more negative influence.

My passion has led me to grow into my purpose which is to help others increase their influence personally and professionally while setting and reaching their goals. I am very passionate and have great conviction. I have realized many benefits by getting better results in all areas of my life. I have improved relationships with my family members, my friends, my associates, my peers, and my clients. I have witnessed people within these same groups embrace leadership principles and reap the same benefits.

The degree to which I *live* what I teach determines my effectiveness. My goal is to learn it, live it, and *then* teach it. I had major internal struggles as I grew my way to where I am. I'm a long way from perfect, so I seek daily improvement. Too often, I see people teaching leadership but not living what they're teaching. If I teach it, I apply it.

My goal is to be a better leader tomorrow than I am today. I simply have to get out of my own way and lead. I must lead me effectively before I can lead others effectively, not only with acquired knowledge, but also with experience from applying and living the principles.

I'll be transparent with personal stories to help you see how I have applied leadership principles by sharing: How I've struggled. How I've learned. How I've sacrificed. How I've succeeded.

Go beyond highlighting or underlining key points. Take the time to write down your thoughts related to the principle. Write down what you want to change. Write down how you can apply the principle in your life. You may want to consider getting a journal to fully capture your thoughts as you progress through the chapters. What you are thinking as you read is often much more important than what you're reading.

Most importantly, do not focus your thoughts on others. Yes, they need it too. We all need it. I need it. You need it. If you focus outside of yourself, you are missing the very point. Your influence comes from within. Your influence rises and falls based on your choices. You have untapped and unlimited potential waiting to be released. Only you can release it.

You, like everyone else, were born a leader. Let's take a leadership journey together.

(If you enjoyed this Introduction to *Defining Influence*, it is available in paperback and as an eBook on Amazon.com or for a signed copy you can purchase at TopStoryLeadership.com.)

Excerpt from

10 Values of High Impact Leaders

Our values are the foundation upon which we build our character. I'll be sharing 10 values high impact leaders work to master because they know these values will have a tremendous impact on their ability to lead others well. You may be thinking, "Aren't there more than 10 leadership values?" Absolutely! They seem to be endless. And, they are all important. These are simply 10 values I believe are key.

Since leadership is very dynamic, the more values you have been able to internalize and utilize synergistically together, the more effective you will be. The more influence you will have.

"High performing organizations that continuously invest in leadership development are now defining new 21st century leadership models to deal with today's gaps in their leadership pipelines and the new global business environment. These people-focused organizations have generated nearly 60% improved business growth, reported a 66% improvement in bench strength, and showed a 62% improvement in employee retention. And, our research shows that it is not enough to just spend money on leadership training, but rather to follow specific practices that drive accelerated business results." ~ Josh Bersin

Do you want to be a high impact leader?

I believe everyone is a leader, but they are leading at different levels.

I believe everyone can and should lead from *where they are*.

I believe everyone can and should make a high impact.

I believe growth doesn't just happen; we must make it happen.

I believe before you will invest in yourself you must first

believe in yourself.

I believe leaders must believe in their team before they will invest in their team.

I truly believe *everything rises and falls on influence.*

There is a story of a tourist who paused for a rest in a small town in the mountains. He went over to an old man sitting on a bench in front of the only store in town and inquired, "Friend, can you tell me something this town is noted for?"

"Well," replied the old man, "I don't rightly know except it's the starting point to the world. You can start here and go anywhere you want."

That's a great little story. We are all at "the starting point" to the world, and we "can start here and go anywhere we want." We can expand our influence 360° in all directions by starting in the center with ourselves.

Consider the following illustration. Imagine you are standing in the center. You can make a high impact. However, it will not happen by accident. You must become intentional. You must live with purpose while focusing on your performance as you develop your potential.

Note: Illustration and 10 Values are listed on the following pages.

Why we do what we do is about our *purpose*.

How we do what we do is about our *performance*.

What we do will determine our *potential*.

Where these three components overlap, you will achieve a
HIGH IMPACT.

10 Values of High Impact Leaders

1

THE VALUE OF VISION
Vision is the foundation of hope.
"When there's hope in the future, there's power in the present." ~ Les Brown

2

THE VALUE OF MODELING
Someone is always watching you.
"Who we are on the inside is what people see on the outside." ~ Mack Story

3

THE VALUE OF RESPONSIBILITY
When we take responsibility, we take control.
"What is common sense is not always common practice." ~ Dr. Stephen R. Covey

4

THE VALUE OF TIMING
It matters when you do what you do.
"It's about doing the right thing for the right reason at the right time." ~ Mack Story

5

THE VALUE OF RESPECT
To be respected, we must be respectful.
"Go See, ask why, and show respect"
~ Jim Womack

6

THE VALUE OF EMPOWERMENT
Leaders gain influence by
giving it to others.
"Leadership is not reserved for leaders."
~ Marcus Buckingham

7

THE VALUE OF DELEGATION
We should lead with questions
instead of directions.
"Delegation 101: Delegating 'what to do,' makes
you responsible. Delegating 'what to accomplish,'
allows others to become responsible."
~ Mack Story

8

THE VALUE OF MULTIPLICATION
None of us is as influential as all of us.
"To add growth, lead followers. To multiply, lead
leaders." ~ John C. Maxwell

9

THE VALUE OF RESULTS
Leaders like to make things happen.
"Most people fail in the getting started."
~ Maureen Falcone

10

THE VALUE OF SIGNIFICANCE
Are you going to settle for success?
"Significance is a choice that only successful people can make."
~ Mack Story

ABOUT RIA STORY

Mack's wife, Ria, is also a motivational leadership speaker, author, and a world class coach who has a unique ability to help people develop and achieve their life and career goals, and guide them in building the habits and discipline to achieve their personal view of greatness. Ria brings a wealth of personal experience in working with clients to achieve their personal goals and aspirations in a way few coaches can.

Like many, Ria has faced adversity in life. Raised on an isolated farm in Alabama, she suffered extreme sexual abuse by her father from age 12 to 19. Desperate to escape, she left home at 19 without a job, a car, or even a high school diploma. Ria learned to be resilient, and not just survive, but thrive. She worked her way through school, acquiring an MBA with a 4.0 GPA, and eventually resigned from her career in the corporate world to pursue a passion for helping others achieve success.

Ria's background includes more than 10 years in healthcare administration, including several years in management, and later, Director of Compliance and Regulatory Affairs for a large healthcare organization. Ria's responsibilities included oversight of thousands of organizational policies, organizational compliance with all State and Federal regulations, and responsibility for several million dollars in Medicare appeals.

Ria co-founded Top Story Leadership, which offers leadership development, speaking, training, coaching, and consulting.

Ria's Story From Ashes to Beauty
by Ria Story

The unforgettable story and inspirational memoir of a young woman who was extremely sexually abused by her father from age 12 to 19 and then rejected by her mother.

For the first time, Ria publicly reveals details of the extreme sexual abuse she endured growing up. 13 years after leaving home at 19, she decided to speak out about her story and encourage others to find hope and healing.

Determined to not only survive, but also thrive, Ria shares how she was able to overcome the odds and find hope and healing to Achieve Abundant Life. She shares the leadership principles she applied to find professional success, personal significance, and details how she was able to find the courage to share her story to give hope to others around the world.

Ria states, *"It would be easier for me to let this story go untold forever and simply move on with life...One of the most difficult things I've ever done is write this book. Victims of sexual assault or abuse don't want to talk because they want to avoid the social stigma and the fear of not being believed or the possibility of being blamed for something that was not their fault. My hope and prayer is someone will benefit from learning how I was able to overcome such difficult circumstances. That brings purpose to the pain and reason enough to share what I would rather have left behind forever. Our scars make us stronger."*

Available at Amazon.com in paperback and eBook.

To order your signed copy, to learn more about Ria, or to book her to speak at your event, please visit:

www.TopStoryLeadership.com

Order books online at Amazon or
www.TopStoryLeadership.com

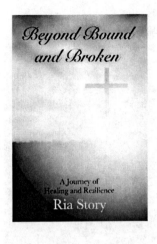

Ria's Story
From Ashes To Beauty

Ria Story

In *Beyond Bound and Broken,* Ria shares how she overcame the shame, fear, and doubt she developed after enduring years of extreme sexual abuse by her father. Forced to play the role of a wife and even shared with other men due to her father's perversions, Ria left home at 19 without a job, a car, or even a high-school diploma. This book also contains lessons on resilience and overcoming adversity that you can apply to your own life.

In *Ria's Story From Ashes To Beauty,* Ria tells her personal story of growing up as a victim of extreme sexual abuse from age 12 – 19, leaving home to escape, and her decision to tell her story. She shares her heart in an attempt to help others overcome their own adversity.

Order books online at Amazon or
www.TopStoryLeadership.com

Note: Leadership Gems is the generic, non-gender specific, version of Leadership Gems for Women. The content is very similar.

Women are naturally high level leaders because they are relationship oriented. However, it's a "man's world" out there and natural ability isn't enough to help you be successful as a leader. You must be intentional.

Ria packed these books with 30 leadership gems which very successful people internalize and apply. Ria has combined her years of experience in leadership roles of different organizations along with years of studying, teaching, training, and speaking on leadership to give you these 30, short and simple, yet powerful and profound, lessons to help you become very successful, regardless of whether you are in a formal leadership position or not.

Order books online at Amazon or
www.TopStoryLeadership.com

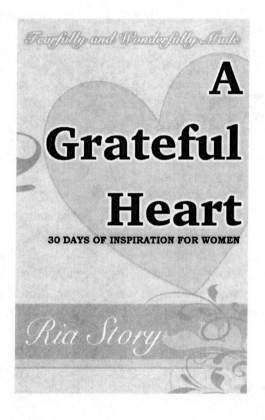

Become inspired by this 30-day collection of daily devotions for women, where you will find practical advice on intentionally living with a grateful heart, inspirational quotes, short journaling opportunities, and scripture from God's Word on practicing gratitude.

Order books online at Amazon or
<u>www.TopStoryLeadership.com</u>

Ria's *Effective Leadership Series* books are written to develop and enhance your leadership skills, while also helping you increase your abilities in areas like communication and relationships, time management, planning and execution, leading and implementing change. Look for more books in the *Effective Leadership Series*:

- *Straight Talk: The Power of Effective Communication*

- *PRIME Time: The Power of Effective Planning*

- *Change Happens: Leading Yourself and Others through Change (Co-authored by Ria & Mack Story)*

Order books online at Amazon or
www.TopStoryLeadership.com

MACK STORY

10 Values of High Impact Leaders

D e m y s t i f y i n g
L e a d e r s h i p   S e r i e s

High impact leaders align their habits with key values in order to maximize their influence. High impact leaders intentionally grow and develop themselves in an effort to more effectively grow and develop others.

These *10 Values* are commonly understood. However, they are not always commonly practiced. These *10 Values* will help you build trust and accelerate relationship building. Those mastering these *10 Values* will be able to lead with speed as they develop 360° of influence from wherever they are.

Order books online at Amazon or
www.TopStoryLeadership.com

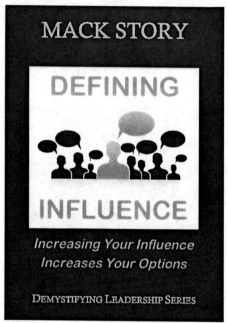

Are you looking for transformation in your life? Do you want better results? Do you want stronger relationships?

In *Defining Influence*, Mack breaks down many of the principles that will allow anyone at any level to methodically and intentionally increase their positive influence.

Mack blends his personal growth journey with lessons on the principles he learned along the way. He's not telling you what he learned after years of research, but rather what he learned from years of application and transformation. Everything rises and falls on influence.

Order books online at Amazon or
www.TopStoryLeadership.com

10 Foundational Elements of Intentional Transformation serves as a source of motivation and inspiration to help you climb your way to the next level and beyond as you learn to intentionally create a better future for yourself. The pages will ENCOURAGE, ENGAGE, and EMPOWER you as you become more focused and intentional about moving from where you are to where you want to be.

All of us are somewhere, but most of us want to be somewhere else. However, we don't always know how to get there. You will learn how to intentionally move forward as you learn to navigate the 10 foundational layers of transformation.

Order books online at Amazon or
www.TopStoryLeadership.com

"Sales persuasion and influence, moving others, has changed more in the last 10 years than it has in the last 100 years. It has transitioned from buyer beware to seller beware" ~ *Daniel Pink*

So, it's no longer "Buyer beware!" It's "Seller beware!" Why? Today, the buyer has the advantage over the seller. Most often, they are holding it in their hand. It's a smart phone. They can learn everything about your product before they meet you. They can compare features and prices instantly. The major advantage you do still have is: YOU! IF they like you. IF they trust you. IF they feel you want to help them.

This book is filled with 30 short chapters providing unique insights that will give you the advantage, not over the buyer, but over your competition: those who are selling what you're selling. It will help you sell yourself.

Order books online at Amazon or
www.TopStoryLeadership.com

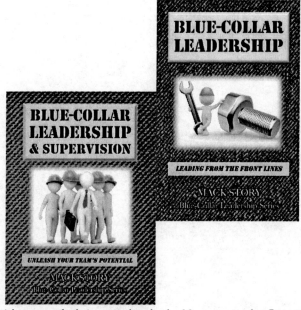

"I wish someone had given me these books 30 years ago when I started my career on the front lines. They would have changed my life then. They can change your life now." ~ Mack Story

Note: These two Blue-Collar Leadership books are the blue-collar version of the MAXIMIZE books and contain nearly identical content.

Blue-Collar Leadership & Supervision and *Blue-Collar Leadership* are written specifically for those who lead the people on the frontlines and for those on the front lines. With 30 short, easy to read 3 page chapters, these books contain powerful, yet simple to understand leadership lessons.

Down load the first 5 chapters now at:
www.BlueCollarLeaders.com

Order books online at Amazon or
www.TopStoryLeadership.com

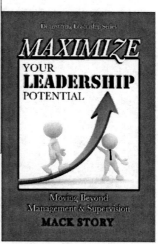

"I wish someone had given me these books 30 years ago when I started my career. They would have changed my life then. They can change your life now." ~ Mack Story

Note: These two MAXIMIZE books are the white-collar, or non-specific, version of the Blue-Collar Leadership books and contain nearly identical content.

MAXIMIZE Your Potential will help you learn to lead yourself well. *MAXIMIZE Your Leadership Potential* will help you learn to lead others well. With 30 short, easy to read 3 page chapters, these books contain simple and easy to understand, yet powerful leadership lessons.

CPSIA information can be obtained
at www.ICGtesting.com
Printed in the USA
FSOW02n1049220817
37874FS